Advance Praise for

EXTRAORDINARY POWER
OF BEING AVERAGE

Demonstrates just how special 'average' can be"
—**Gregory Hendy**, MDChief Emergency Medicine, UCLA

The Extraordinary Power of Being Average is a must-read
for medical professionals and average humans! Written by
an exceptional doctor and even greater human being. The
overwhelming message of Mel's story is practical, inclusive,
and kind: "Average people from humble beginnings go on
to do extraordinary things."

—**Juli Boit**, Founder, Living Room International
Author, From Beyond the Skies & Brave Love

FROM THE INTERNATIONALLY APPLAUDED
TALK THAT FORMS THE BASIS OF THIS BOOK:

You managed to convert a broken, hopeless heart into
a heart that pulsates in other people's lives. That's a
superhero.

@abutony1195

Fantastic pep talk. Thanks for rejuvenating my burnt
out spirit in medicine.

@averysrevelries7673

Moving talk, truly amazing! Thank you for all you have
done and all you continue to do! Hats off to you.

—**Sumera M.**

THE EXTRAORDINARY POWER OF BEING AVERAGE

How a very ordinary kid from outback Australia
became a doctor, created one of the worlds
most successful education programs,
and how being average was the key
to his success and can be yours.

Mel Herbert, MD

Print- 979-8-9900627-2-6(Paperback)
ISBN: 979-8-9900627-1-9 (eBook)

Library of Congress Control Number: *to come*

Book design by Glen Edelstein, Hudson Valley Book Design

Printed in the United States of America.

First printing edition 2024.

*To my amazing wife, remarkable son,
and all of the amazing average people
we work with every day!*

Writing is a form of therapy;
sometimes I wonder how all those who do not write,
compose, or paint can manage to escape the madness,
melancholia, the panic and fear which is inherent
in a human situation.

—Graham Greene

Contents

Preface

IN MY FIVE DECADES ON THIS PLANET, I have been a failed student, a broken child, a wounded man, a physician, an educator, and an entrepreneur. I have created multi-million-dollar education companies, won many awards, and been recognized throughout the medical world. Through all of it, I have always been, and will always be, average. And while some hear that word and conjure up only the most negative connotations—lackluster, unexceptional, mediocre—I beg to differ. Experience has taught me a profound truth that is the simple premise of this book: *Average people have a special power, and if they tap into that power, they can do extraordinary things.*

At times deeply autobiographical, as I am indeed average in all things, this book is also the story of an extraordinary group of people that created one of the most successful medical education companies in the world. Most of these folks, like me, are average, but together and because of that fact, we have created a most wonderful creative environment where excellence thrives. This is my story and, in part, their story. A story of what we have done together and the lessons we have learned.

A word of caution, however: the American author, Mary McCarthy, is oft quoted as saying, "We are (necessarily) the hero of our own story." This is certainly true in this book and in my life. We have to believe we are the heroes of our own stories. But that means we should also have a reasonable amount of skepticism about the accuracy of the details of an autobiographical work such as this, as it is, in fact, written by the hero himself. Consider yourself forewarned.

Finally, to those who think that because of the work I have done and, more importantly, the extraordinary work our team has accomplished together, I am, and we are, therefore, not average, I say you missed the point. I hope to convince you in the following pages, beyond any shadow of a doubt, that I am, and we are, average. And that being average can be your superpower, you just need to know how to use it.

To Do Extraordinary Things

I SUSPECT LIKE MOST PEOPLE I am overly enamored by people who are "successful," in sports, business, science, life in general. They are all around us, these people who seem to have it all worked out. They rise to the top of the pile, they succeed, and that success seems to breed even more success. Over time, they seem to distance themselves from the rest of us in ways and to degrees we cannot imagine. I can't help but wonder how many of them are just average people who did extraordinary things.

Eliud Kipchoge comes to mind here. Considered by everyone in the world to be the greatest marathon runner of all time, he was one of six kids, raised by a single mother, living on a farm. He started out in life running to school like every other average kid, and made himself into the greatest marathon runner of all time. I also think of Howard Schultz, the "re-founder" and longtime CEO of Starbucks who grew up in the projects of Brooklyn, starting out as an appliance salesman and going on to become one of the most successful businessmen in history. Or Rosa Parks, a girl from Tuskegee, Alabama, who could not finish high school because she had to care for her dying grandmother then mother, and who performed an act of defiance that helped ignite a world-wide civil rights movement.

I could go on, story after story, person after person. It is the rule, not the exception, that average people from humble beginnings go on to do extraordinary things. Margaret Mead said, "Never doubt that a small group of thoughtful committed individuals can change the world. In fact, it's the only thing that ever has." Yet, despite hearing these kinds of stories since we were old enough to talk, most of us believe we cannot do extraordinary things because we are, you guessed it, just average. At the risk of repeating myself many, many times, I will say it again: being average is a superpower; you simply need to understand and embrace it, and all things are possible.

Let's go to Boston in 1967 for a moment. The marathon is underway, and a young lady named Kathrine Switzer has decided to run, but there's one problem: women are not allowed to compete. The excuses ranged from women's bodies not being strong enough to run a marathon, to the sight of women running being unsightly and just wrong. *Really.* It was a whole thing, men trying to drag her out of the race. Today, the women's marathon record is two hours, 11 minutes 53 seconds now held by the remarkable Ethiopian runner Tigst Assefa, which would have made her the world record holder for men in the 1960s—when women were considered less than average, not even capable of finishing a marathon. Now, women's times in the marathon are falling faster than men's, leaving one to wonder when their times will equal or exceed them. My point? The idea of average and what is possible is more often a cultural construct than a scientific one.

In another running analogy, the legendary Roger Banister, an avid runner and medical student, broke the four-minute-mile barrier on May 6, 1954, at a time when it was believed physically impossible to run a mile in under four minutes. The prevailing wisdom was that the human body would somehow explode, implode, or just "plode" and you would die. While many people had come close to the magic record, no one had done it before Banister, who remarked that from a physical standpoint, there was no difference between running a four-minute mile and a three-minutes and fifty-nine-second mile. Sometimes, the average is restricted by our imagination.

If you think big, big is possible. Bannister broke the record, and—this is the really interesting part—once this psychological barrier was broken, it was quickly broken time and again. Today, the record stands at three minutes and forty-three seconds by the remarkable Hicham El Guerrouj. Once an average person does something that seems impossible, it often becomes routine. A good number of elite high school athletes can run the mile in under four minutes. Perhaps not routine, but no longer considered impossible. The important thing to remember is that when an average person strives for big, it's amazing what they can accomplish.

Consider for a moment the incomparable success of Tiger Woods and compare it with that of John Daly, a professional golfer who won many titles and two major championships in his time. Tiger Woods suggested that John Daly was perhaps the most naturally gifted golfer he has ever met. Sadly, Daly had a drinking, smoking, and partying problem, and did not like to practice. Woods, though his transgressions and partying are well known, had a ridiculous work ethic and was on the range before and after pretty much every other golfer. Daly would watch him practice, practice, and practice some more while he sat in his van and drank beer. Daly went on to win five PGA tournaments, which is excellent. Woods has won eighty-two.

In this theoretical scenario, two golfers of similar natural ability have vastly different win ratios, with Tiger winning sixteen times as often as his friend John Daly. The difference here is that one of them was willing to apply the practice of delayed gratification to his talent, the other was not. Spending more time on the hard thing and less time on the short-term pleasurable thing allows you to do better at the hard thing. Any average person can practice this pattern and get better and better, perhaps even extraordinary.

Related to this concept is "reversion to the mean," which is the idea that data, events, and people will tend toward an average. For example, let's say you usually shoot eighty-five when playing eighteen holes of golf. Better than a lot of people, not as good as others. This means for nine holes you are generally shooting in the low forties. Let's say one day you shoot a thirty-five on the first nine holes. Reversion to the mean suggests you are not very likely to shoot thirty-five on the next nine, but something much worse, since, over time, your average is a lot higher than that first nine holes.

However, this does not mean you cannot get better. Moving the average for all of us takes a lot of effort, time, and dedication. You might go out and have an off day and shoot a terrible score, but if you have worked yourself up to a sixty-eight average, it is likely that after shooting a "terrible" eighty-two, you will have a good round next time out. You can move your average over time, be it in sports, business, life, anything. Using this knowledge, you can help yourself and others slowly but surely move your game to a higher level. This is how ordinary people come to do extraordinary things.

Embracing the Average

TRYING TO LEARN A LANGUAGE as an adult can be kind of disheartening. Turns out, new language learning gets harder as we get older, especially for those who only speak one language. When I hear of the struggles of friends of mine on the same path, trying to make their middle-aged brains tackle this task, I am inspired. "So, you too have a hard time making these connections! You too get the same Duolingo phrase wrong eight times in a row!" The dear friends who speak multiple languages and can learn more of them over the weekend are lovely people but, in this struggle, they are not particularly helpful. Bring me your average struggling language learners to help me in my path. Turns out, they have great pearls of wisdom and resources. They, like me, have tried everything, and can help me sort the wheat from the chaff. We understand one another's struggle, and know that together we can do this.

Understanding we all struggle from time to time means we have to stop pretending that the Instagram life is our actual life. We need to embrace the idea that by being average, accepting it, sharing it, we will create bonds that go far beyond those made by posting a pretty picture at the beach. The average person seeing that perfectly filtered picture is not inspired, but rather left feeling worse for it. Inspiring is the average person sharing they'd rather not get out of bed and go to work or school that day, then going anyway—haven't we all felt that?

To say that kids today are more stressed, more likely to die by suicide, more likely to have eating disorders, depression, and a host of mental health issues than prior generations is now well known. Social media did the opposite of what its early proponents had hoped; rather than bring us all together, it drove us all apart. Any parent, any adult in general, can prove that by definition, most of us are average. Average looks, height, intelligence, with average motivation and dreams, and that is not at all a bad thing. That is indeed a wonderful and inspiring thing. Rather than hide from it, rather than deny it, accept it, understand the positive of it.

One of my friends always says the key to a happy and successful life is to drop your expectations—a line my friends and I use all the time on the golf course. Once we accept that we are extremely average golfers, and that shot that went flying into the trees is all part of being average, the game becomes a whole lot more fun. By no means does being average stop us from loving the game and trying to get better all the time. Seeing our shots go comically astray is a reminder that we are just some Average Joes having a nice walk and playing a hopelessly hard game.

The real key to success is embracing our averageness, then moving beyond it and using it to relate to those around us. In learning theory, there is this idea that in order to move a piece of information into one's long-term memory you have to go over it a number of times. As a vague rule, most of us need to learn or read or study something at time zero, then again in twenty-four hours, seven days, one month, and one year to make it stick. Knowing I am not the only person who struggles with retention, I incorporated this rule into my teaching and education business.

When interviewing a guest contributor who is introducing a key learning concept for one of our educational videos, I start by simply pointing it out. "Did you hear that? Do you understand this is a key learning point?" During the interview, I summarize these key learning pieces again, even making fun of myself about it. At the end of the interview, I go over these key learning pieces again—what I call giving people "the meat." The next month, we go back to those teaching points and remind people what those meaty chunks were to try and help their long-term retention. This process comes naturally for me because my memory is so average. It is no stretch for me to do this slavishly because it is the only way I can remember things, and knowing that most people listening and watching are average, I know it will be helpful to them. My averageness made our education above average.

I have been lucky to receive numerous education awards in my life at various levels, from universities, trade organizations, students and residents and international education groups. A fact I have always found funny, due to an exceptional number of poop jokes to my credit and the fact that, as an average student, I just repeat the s$%t out of things so people have an easier time remembering. The awards would suggest I am an excellent teacher—not really, I am an average learner. I teach from the assumption that most people are just like me. Not so much exceptional as a little insightful and helpful.

I never simply accepted myself as "being average," I used it to make a big part of my career successful. Starting out with average beginnings and, over time, realizing that most people around me were about at my level, helped me accomplish things in my work I never thought possible. This is the power of being average. I assure you, most people are just like you. Use that knowledge to help yourself, and others, become extraordinary.

Average Beginnings in Oz

I LOVED RURAL AUSTRALIA, THE home where I grew up in the 1960s and 70s. The land was dry, burnt dry, from long hot summers and drought, but still exceptionally beautiful. Kangaroos abounded—see what I did there?—and even today find a way to thrive in this majestic landscape. Danger lurked everywhere, in the form of a snake, a spider, or another snake—as eight of the world's most poisonous snakes live there. It was a place that seemed to want to kill the humans at every turn, but to me, that's not how it felt. It felt like home. My childhood was the perfect setup for an average upbringing. The kind most of us, by statistical rule, will have. Yet, there was power in those early years, power in the very averageness of it all.

Mine was not an idyllic, carefree childhood. Like most, I expect, it was complicated. Some aspects of it were good, and some were sad, angry, and violent at times, reflecting the community I grew up in. I lived in rural Australia until I was about fourteen, going to the local public school where, let's just say, I was not the best student. Our farm was three miles from a town of about a hundred and fifty people with a central school that took in students from across the district. Our community felt cut off from the magic of big city life, with its movies and technology and places of learning. Many were plagued by the nagging feeling that we were not equal to those big-city folks. And since rural life comes with the added bonus of endless hours with nothing much to do, we experienced things like drugs, drinking, sex, and depression with more frequency.

There were five of us kids—three brothers and one sister and, as a friend once said, we had "one of each." I would like to give you a wonderful dissertation of *each*, with great insights, humorous stories, and my vast understanding of why we all turned out like we did, but I will not. What one writes of the living, especially in one's family, is usually one-sided, poorly thought through and executed, and will no doubt lead to serious trouble. Trouble I'd like to avoid. I'll just say this: all of us are survivors of a terrible childhood and an abusive father who left his scars. We did not all survive and thrive. Some of us just survived.

While my siblings and I shared the same family, family order no doubt meant our experiences of childhood were very different. The years between our ages alone mean that what was one child's experience was not others. I think my older siblings experienced a time when my mother was more dominant, smoothing out the worst part of my father. Those of us later in the birth order experienced my father as the dominant figure and a mother that had retreated. All of us agreed that our father was terribly difficult and abusive. A rage machine we all feared and tried to placate.

Aside from my mother, the one thing my father was obsessed with was his business, or in his case, businesses. He owned a variety of companies and businesses in the course of his life. While he was a hard worker, seven days a week, morning till night, and desperately wanted to be rich, he was a serial, usually failed, entrepreneur. The one successful business he had he sold in his mid-thirties for a tidy sum that allowed him to move to the country and buy a five-thousand-acre farm with all the various toys. With essentially no experience of how to run a farm, he went all in. But this, too, eventually went broke. After about twelve years, during a terrible drought that destroyed many farmers at the time, he gave up and we moved back to the city.

In Melbourne, he got into business with an old friend who ran a company that made growth material for bacteria. The partnership did not last long and my father ended up with the entire company, then spent the next few decades trying to make it work. Since we could walk, we kids were commanded to work in his businesses—before school, after school, weekends, holidays, whenever he felt we were needed, which was pretty much all the time. My father believed that if you were not working you were slacking, and if you were not working you must be a "socialist." His conversations with us were always about work: we must do this or that for "the business," as in, get up at five a.m. or take out another loan. There was always this idea that one day he would hit it big, get rich, and all this work would be worthwhile.

As kids, we all hated that business, and hated all it represented: a loss of childhood, no fun, no games, no after-school sports, no normal childhood. Perhaps we hated that he clearly loved the business more than his children and that we were only as good as the work we could do for him and it. There was no joy in it, no feeling we were all in it together. He made us feel bad about it; he yelled and screamed and told us how stupid we were, how smart he was, and if we grumbled, we were lazy, you guessed it, socialists.

However, being an average kid in that situation was a spectacular motivation. I used the energy that came from wanting to get out to do above-average things. I am the fourth of five kids and got to watch my older siblings make some pretty serious life decisions that I would learn deeply from. The single biggest mistake they made in my opinion was to continue to work for my father. I was young enough to see how "working for Dad " was not a good game plan. So, while I was sweeping floors, screwing on bottle caps, mixing up chemicals that stank to high hell, I was also being vaccinated against ever doing that work long term. One way or the other, I would find a way out.

Our father is the one family member no longer living and they say you should not talk ill of the dead, but I call bullshit on that. He was eccentric, angry, manipulative, egotistical, violent, smart (though not as smart as he thought he was), entrepreneurial, an emotional terrorist and just plain broken. He was the most emotionally, and in our early years, physically abusive person I had ever known. It did not, he did not, completely destroy us, but came damn close for most of us.

In Jimmy Barnes' first book, *Working Class Boy*, the Australian icon and Hall of Fame rocker describes a similar kind of violence, anger, alcoholism, sadness and rage in his relationship with his father. My father, like his, broke me, made me feel small, stupid, and useless since as far back as I can remember. Made me feel like I could never measure up, never be worthy of his love. Made me try, day after day, moment after moment, to keep him calm, to prevent him from exploding with his spectacular rage. I hated that rage; I hated that father.

Sometimes hating the life you are born into becomes the very motivation you need to get out. It becomes the fire that lights up your night, that helps you get up early and work late so that one day, you don't have to get up early and work late. To rise above one's circumstance requires work, effort, often a fairly relentless amount of both. In my experience, the difference between people who achieve exceptional things and those who don't is much less about them being exceptional and much more about them being relentless. The good news here is even the most average person from a broken background can be relentless. It requires practice and a little delayed gratification. Use that energy, the positive or the negative, and be relentless. Over time, it will pay dividends.

Less Than Average Childhood

AVERAGE PEOPLE COME, IN GENERAL, from average families. That is to say, there is some good, some bad, and lots in between in family life. Though I consider myself average, my childhood was less than stellar, my person, my psyche, seriously damaged. In this sense, I might be called significantly below average. While my father saw to it that we were put down, belittled, shamed, and made to feel like a constant disappointment, our mother, so good in many ways, so very much needed to protect us from him, was often simply not there. And since the only two things our father really cared about were our mother and his business, it was not even a question in our minds that we were simply a byproduct of the marriage, something to be tolerated.

My mother, who as of this writing is still alive but nearing her end, is a kind person, a sweet person whom people liked. She was, in her time, quite the beauty and quite the delight of the Irish clubs in Melbourne with her flowing red hair and a wonderful singing voice. She was also one of the most terribly damaged people I have ever known and because of it, unable to be the mother I am sure she would have liked to have been. My experience of her as a child was largely one of looking for a mother who was never quite there.

When we were growing up, my mother was fragile and we were told all the time by our father that she had a "condition," a "hormonal" thing. Once triggered, this condition could send her into days of being semi-comatose and unable to communicate, retreating to her room. During less severe attacks, she would just get a little mean, with an edge, a sarcasm made amplified by the fact that this was just not her personality. We knew something dark lurked in her past, and that this caused her condition. We were told by our father to leave her alone, to not bother her, not upset her, or we would feel the full extent of his wrath. That wrath, when we were smaller kids, was physical or verbal, the back of his hand sent me flying across the room many times.

As a child, these episodes my mother had were terrifying for me. I had no idea what they were, what to do with them. My mother was gone, the explanation vague. I learned early on she could not be relied upon, she could not explain the world, could not metabolize our fears. She did not know how and, what's more, she had a husband who would not even let her try. Theirs was a classic co-dependent relationship, and having lived it as a child, I can tell you it was very destructive.

I have vivid memories of the many traumas this broken mother-child bond created. Once, when I was ten years old, my mother and I drove about thirty minutes to the store, and on the way back, the car broke down. This was 1970s rural Australia, the roads were dirt, the cars not so great, and breaking down was a thing that seemed to happen about half the time you drove more than ten miles. So, we limped into a stranger's front driveway where I figured my mother would get out, knock on the door, explain the situation, and have me wait in the car with her until help arrived. Not so. I was sent in to ask the owners to call our home, have someone from the farm come and get us, and maybe tow the car. I did what I was told—knocked on the door and presented the request, to my terrible introverted embarrassment.

Then it got worse: she sent me back to check on the progress every ten minutes or so. Each time I went to the door I wanted to die, to become invisible. Some hours later, one of the farm "hands" came in the ute (pickup) to bring us home. At this point, my mother was near unconscious, and when he asked what was wrong with her, I explained it was a thing that sometimes happened, some hormonal thing. To which he said words to the effect of, "Bullshit, she's fucking pissed out of her mind." Pissed, in this instance, being Australian for drunk, semi-unconscious drunk. You can imagine my surprise, my confusion. I knew what drunk was, how could she be drunk? I occasionally saw her have a glass of wine at dinner, but never drunk. In my ten-year-old mind, this could simply not be true.

Another time, one of my father's workers needed a check signed, and my father was away—he was pretty much always away during these episodes. The worker asked me to have my mother sign a check for him. I went into her room and she refused, I went out, he told me to go back in. Here I was again, a little kid being ping-ponged between two adults ever more agitated at me and I did not know what the hell was going on. My mother finally relented and signed a check for him. The signature was unintelligible, I was sure he'd refuse to accept it, but he took it anyway.

Rather than a safe haven from my terrorist father, my mother was part of the torment in our lives, placing us in terrible positions, adding to our insecurity, further deepening our wounds.

It was only many years later that these episodes were explained by the fact that our mother was indeed an alcoholic, had been since she was a young woman, and it had defined her adult life. The reason she was an alcoholic was the real tragedy. For my mother, drinking was self-medication, nothing more or less than that. Sparing you the horrible details, my mother was terribly sexually and physically abused. It is unimaginable to me the pain and suffering and scarring this must have caused. How she was even the slightest bit functional, I will never know. Drinking was her way to blunt the pain.

Sadly, because my mother was so broken and unable to care for herself, she did not protect us, could not protect us, from my father's violence and emotional terrorism. She did not have the energy for it. Her energy, her sense of self, had been irrevocably damaged. Her childhood, like mine, was a dumpster fire, a fire that left the very foundations of her life unstable to the end.

Those of us who grew up with abusive or absent parents know firsthand how difficult a less-than average childhood is to overcome. Yet, there is a remarkable energy that comes with it. What we do with that energy makes all the difference in the kind of lives we lead. In my experience, it can go either of two ways: a lifetime of self-destruction, or a furnace for great, great productivity. Or, I suspect in most cases, a period of self-destruction and then resolution, and hopefully great productivity. Or, more likely, both energy for success and failure that occurs on and off throughout one's life. I have seen that energy destroy one brother and leave him in federal prison. I have seen it make me do more work and study harder than I could have imagined. If one can overcome the destructive part, the part that makes you believe you're so far below average you'll never see above it, you can do great things.

The Wounded Healer

MY SIBLINGS AND I SURVIVED our childhood, but only just. We each have our own issues with anger, depression, anxiety, and/or substance abuse, but we "survived." In writing about these painful years, I am reminded of one of the most powerful scenes in cinematic history from one of my favorite movies of all time. In *Good Will Hunting*, the psychiatrist played by Robin Williams hugs the terribly abused and broken main character played by Matt Damon. After trying to break through to his genius, the psychiatrist says to the young man, "It's not your fault, it's not your fault." The pain, the tears, the heaving, the sheer weight of the thing, the terrible thing his childhood left him, is felt by all. The pain, but also the sense of palpable hope in that scene is what gets me. Hope that something good could come from so much pain.

I have spent many hours in therapy trying to tease out the elements of my broken childhood and I keep coming back to the same questions: Why was my father such an

A-hole? Why was he so angry? Why was he so abusive to his children? I have never found the answers. His parents, my grandparents, seemed like nice, good people. I know my father didn't like his father—he felt he wasn't good enough for his mother, that he had held her back. And he harbored quite the Oedipus complex regarding his mother. Was this where the rage came from somehow? I don't know and I'll never know, and in the end, I guess it doesn't matter.

Perhaps if I knew I'd have this great sense of relief in being able to say, "That's why he was such an ass, now I can forgive him." And, of course, I have tried to forgive him, as carrying the weight of it is too much, too destructive. But the energy, the brokenness, always remains. My wife said it best: in her life, whatever happened growing up, she knew her parents deeply loved her and cared for her and would always have her back. This became the foundation of her life, her very self. I did not have that, so like a ship without an anchor, some fundamental part of me has always felt adrift. Full of anxiety and melancholy and energy. Energy that can be targeted to productivity, but also energy that can eat itself.

This lack of self-love, self-regard, is a dangerous thing. It can result in depression, death by suicide, or in never being able to have long-term relationships. It's cliché, but if you don't first love yourself, you cannot be loved by others. You will always have this terrible voice saying *They don't really love me, I am unlovable.* This is so destructive, and though subtle to the outside world, it is very real and damaging to one's inner world.

I have suffered from this since childhood, but only in later adulthood through time, therapy, and crisis, have I come to realize the impact of it. Perhaps all of this activity I have surrounded myself with, all of this work I've done, all of this "achieving" has been driven by a desire to give myself meaning. To give myself the self-esteem my childhood did not. This in itself is not a bad thing, as long as the work is important. If it is "good," it can be a force for useful change, like jujitsu, turning the weakness to strength. But it's not sufficient to bring healing and closure. In the end, lots of work—in the form of therapy—is needed, but not time alone.

Amita Trasi wrote, "It is said that time heals everything. I don't think that's true. As the years have gone by, I've found it odd how simple things can still remind you of those terrible times or how the moment you try so hard to forget becomes your sharpest memory." It's not enough to wait for time to heal wounds, we must go about the work of healing them. Yes, that will take time, but time alone is not and never has been sufficient.

There is, however, an unexpected gift that comes with being broken, which is that you find yourself in the position of being a wounded healer. The concept of the wounded healer isn't new, but it's an important one in my own story. In Henry Nouwen's beautifully written book, *The Wounded Healer,* he describes a concept made famous by Carl Jung, which is that a therapist is compelled to help patients because they themselves are broken. This concept can be extended to all of us. It is certainly true of me; perhaps my entire motivation to become a physician was to help others because I myself was so broken. It certainly has felt that way and been very helpful in my professional life.

In the Emergency Department we see many broken people, self-medicating with drugs and alcohol, often parts of their bodies and minds missing from gangs and a life of violence. I look at these people and think: that could be me. One more abusive day with my father and I could have easily moved from medical student to drug addict. The rage and sadness that fuel the broken can easily turn on itself at any time. I still fear it to this day, and feel incredibly lucky to have made it this far.

It is a fact that someone's brokenness, the self-loathing they carry from a terrible childhood, can become their most positive characteristic. Consider this: the world sees a homeless person on the street shooting heroin, lying in their own excrement, and sees failure, sadness, and a threat. That person has lost some essential human characteristics like self-care and concern, as the drugs have hijacked their brain. That need for drugs can make them do terrible things, and that person can become quite dangerous. The world, therefore, quite reasonably, fears and even hates them.

You, the average person, the broken person, however, can see more. You see how that person could be you. The sadness, the brokenness, the violence that made them try and escape their lives through drugs, you know that place. They could easily have been you. You look down and see not the "other," but a story in a parallel universe that could easily have been yours. Luck or a subtle change of circumstance is the only difference between the two universes. That recognition of shared brokenness leads to compassion, and compassion can make you a remarkably average, magnificent, wounded healer.

In that sense, Henry Nouwen's premise of the wounded healer does not go far enough. I would suggest you don't have to be wounded to be a great healer. It helps, but just being average is sufficient for helping heal so many things. Who among us has not done a really stupid thing, said the worst, most inappropriate words at the worst possible time? You look back on those things and cringe with more than a minor dose of self-loathing. The average person's struggles are near universal. You are the wounded healer, perhaps without the wounds, you are, simply by being human, able to relate to and help heal those around you.

Take, for instance, the average teenager who has experienced acne, that simple, non-life-threatening skin condition that's one of the most underrated causes of insecurity in the teenage years. You feel like a leper, afraid to go out and be seen, afraid of the bully calling it out. That condition, so common and usually transient, can do real damage to a person's ego. It is little solace that these difficult times, these painfully average acne times, can one day make you a superhero in the empathy department. You will be able to say to the kid with the acne just like yours: life will go one, it gets better, skin will clear up. The beautiful, confident, clear-skinned teen will have a hard time relating to the kid who finds it hard to get up in the morning and face the day, and especially the classroom, with all their anxieties and in-securities.

The wounded healer is the average person who, hav-ing survived the human spectrum of average-to-crappy experiences, can now pass down a ladder to help those around them out of the pit. They can save lives like some kind of a superhero, while only being, in most cases, just average. Look around you at all the people who could benefit from your story, your healing. Do not be afraid to share the pain, to hear their stories. The best way to open the door to their healing is to tell them your story. Let your average life be the door to letting them share theirs.

Wake-Up Call

FOR AN AVERAGE STUDENT WITH average ability, getting into medical school is pretty spectacularly hard. If you had looked at my transcripts through primary and middle school years, you would be impressed at just how bad they were. I mean, really impressed. I failed at everything. School was a place to have fun, to try and make everyone laugh, not a place to learn anything. I pursued my lack of education with some rigor. Getting in trouble constantly, failing wonderfully, having a marvelous time while hiding from the pain and fear of home. Except in science. I liked science, I did reasonably well in science, and that would play out well in the future.

In the late 1970s, high school was looming and it was make-it-or-break-it time for me. My older siblings had all been sent to boarding school, and that had been a spectacular disaster. Like me, they were not academically inclined and living on the farm was their soul, their focus, their being. To be sent off to a Catholic boarding school hours from home was a special type of torture. My father thought the religious "brothers" could smack some sense into his boys and put in the time to educate them where he had failed. My brothers went and they hated it. One made it his project to get kicked out of the place, and though my other brother was less disruptive, he never finished. I think his constant pleading to my parents finally had an effect.

There was talk of me being sent to this school. At this point, I was pretty much beaten down, never speaking back to my father for fear of the rage machine and the very large back of this hand. A hand those blows had, at many times, literally made me piss myself. I was, however, not going to this place—no way, no how, it was not going to happen. My brothers' stories convinced me I was not going to this rape-y, weird boarding school, thank you very much. I made it very clear to my father if I went there, I would just leave. I would do zero work. I would bring as much shame on him and the family as I could. To my surprise, it worked.

So, another plan arose. About forty-five minutes away was a much bigger town than ours, with a few thousand people and a few high schools considered much better than the central school where I was. Arrangements were made to go and speak with the principals. Transcripts in hand, my mother took me to meet these esteemed educators. I was particularly stressed, about to be judged and given the thumbs up or down. Added to that was the fact that I really did not want to go. I wanted to stay with the friends I had known since kindergarten. In this scenario, I would remain on the farm and go to one of these schools with some of the kids I grew up with. So, in the scheme of things, it was better than the Catholic boarding school nightmare. Despite all of this, I was not excited and it didn't go well.

The principal, a woman whose name I have long forgotten, the life no doubt very long gone from her, was quite direct. After reading my report cards and the comments of my teachers, the summary was simple: "Your son is a troublemaker! We have plenty of those here already, we don't need any more." At which point, I burst into tears and the principal, taken aback, stared at my mother. A common misconception is that "the troublemaker" is rough and tough, their defenses strong and well-fortified. Of course, the real story is usually much sadder. In my case, I think it was a cry for help. I did not want to be seen as just another wayward kid from the outback, destined to never finish school, to be angry and like so many I saw ahead of me, never quite knowing what to do next. Football, beer, fights, abuse, and depression was the future I saw coming. This principle, in one quick statement, called me out and it hurt. I wanted to be good, to do well in school, to make something of my life. No one in my immediate family had finished high school. Being a tool at school was the model I had, and I was trying to be really good at it.

How do you rise above the average when simply trying to do so would make you a target? Where I grew up, if you were good at school and got good marks, you were an asshole, uppity, tall poppy, worthy of scorn, abuse, and generally made to be "other." My frail psyche could never take that; I needed my friends, I needed to be part of the tribe. Did this principal know any of this, did she care? Or was she just like my father, completely convinced you are what you were from the moment you were born. If he decided he didn't like you, there was no redemption possible, you were a loser, "just like your Uncle X or Y." One brother, he decided, was the biggest loser of all, completely without hope, and that brother made it his life's work to prove him correct. With a combination of drugs, alcohol, and violence, eventually ending up in jail on a variety of charges including assault with a deadly weapon.

Yes, that principal broke me down, but it was also a wake-up call. When I was bawling my head off, she threw me a lifeline. She suggested, if not in these exact terms, that if I could get my shit together at my current school for the next term, turn my scores around, and most importantly, "Shut the hell up and listen, and not try to be disruptive every two seconds," she would give me a second look.

That moment in her office has stayed with me all these years, making me more empathetic to the kids I see who are struggling. My automatic assumption with these so-called troublemakers is not "This kid is forever screwed, no good to the bone." Rather, the empathy of a broken childhood creates a different picture, a different question: "I wonder what the hell is going on in that kid's home?" The ability to ask different questions, to see more than what's on the surface, is only possible if you have been misjudged, sized up, measured, and found less than average. It's something you never forget.

A Second Chance for the Below Average

HAVING BEEN GIVEN THIS SECOND chance, what was I to do? At twelve or thirteen, I generally didn't have much insight, but I knew wanted to be worthy of that second chance. So, the most disruptive kid in class went on a self-imposed smartass lockdown. Rather than make a stupid comment about every word association that came into my head, I shut up and listened. I asked actual questions. I may have even done actual homework. Maybe. I was determined to turn this puppy around. To show this principal that I could actually be a functioning member of a classroom.

Turns out, it didn't matter what that principal thought of my miraculous transformation, as we were about to move away from the farm and to the big city—Melbourne, at the time probably three million people or so—and it sucked in the most spectacular way. I suddenly found myself on the receiving end of the worst bullying I'd ever experienced. I was a country hick now in the big city, a fish out of water about to discover how incredibly tribal people can be, kids in particular.

There are many forms of "othering" we might face, no matter who we are. From the color of our skin, to the sex chromosomes we carry, the region we find ourselves a part of, or the size of our ears. People, kids in particular, are incredibly tribal. If we think it will make us more popular, less likely to be attacked or estranged from the group, we will do pretty terrible things. We will bully and name call and, just as bad, allow bullying and name calling.

I wanted to go to public school, of which there were many, but my father had it in his head that the only way forward was for me to go to a "real" school——a private school, where I could be forced to try and make something of myself. Oddly, though my father was adamant about me making it into a university, he spent hours a day ranting about the "bullshit" they teach there. He was one of those people who desperately wanted to be part of a club that he never got to join and because of it, spent his life rallying against them.

In Australia at the time, single-sex private schools did indeed have an outsized portal to the university system. If you wanted to go to medical school, then a private, all-boys school was the most likely way to do it. There were so many interviews, I lost count. All of them ending the same: rejection. These schools would have nothing to do with me. I was a country kid, clearly with some serious issues and a pretty terrible academic history. What I do remember were the drives home with my father telling me what a loser I was, yet again.

As fate would have it, however, one principal in one school somehow saw potential in this country bumpkin. The usual routine was gone through: my report cards handed over, parents trying to explain I was not a complete loss. Except this principal looked up and said, "You like science?" I answered that indeed I did. I really, really liked it. To which the principal said, in summary, that the fact that I could get a good grade in one topic showed I was not stupid, which I took as a partially kind insight. We also got talking about PE, which I also liked, especially gymnastics. Turns out, this new school had an excellent gymnastics team, one that had been to the state finals many times. I was beyond excited. Clearly, the principal saw this spark and made me a deal. He would accept me into the school, I could go try out for the team, but if I fell back into my smartass ways, I would be booted in seriously quick fashion.

It is no understatement to say that this man, this principal, changed my life forever. He saw what others had not, and was prepared to give me a chance. No one else wanted me, yet he saw in me some possibility, a spark, and he held out his hand and pulled me out of the pit. Without him looking at this spectacularly less-than-average student, and despite this, giving me a chance, I am not sure where I would be today. I suspect I would have made my way back to the country, become disillusioned, alcoholic, depressed, and ended up like so many of my relatives, dead well before my time. I thank you, sir, with all my heart.

If you have even been given a chance, despite not being stellar, despite your shortcomings, you get it. There's a humility that comes with receiving compassion from another human being, especially someone in a position of power over you, who could have just as easily overlooked your potential. When you've been on the receiving end of that kind of a chance—whether it's your first, second, or tenth—you can't help but feel more compassionate toward others in the same boat as you once were. You come away from that experience with more depth, insight, and empathy. Once again, proving that average is your superpower.

Tribes, Bullies, and Kindness

THERE I WAS, COUNTRY BUMPKIN, fresh off the boat, thrown into a private all-boys school with exactly zero friends and no idea how that little world worked. Turns out, it worked like much of the rest of the world. You guessed it, tribal. I was about to get schooled, not only in Math, Science, and History, but on the finer points as well as the painful ones, of tribal mentality.

The dominant and largest tribe was the group of kids who had gone to primary and middle school together and then moved on up to high school (grades seven through twelve), a majority of whom were also part of some pretty wealthy families. I do not want to disparage the well-off—turns out, now I am one of them—but it can be true that growing up with money, going to private school, being surrounded by people with money at said private schools can make a subset of those people, well, assholes. There's a reason they have been stereotyped in books and movies from the beginning of time. The king's

37

kids often turn out to be privileged tossers (an exceptionally useful Australian/British term). My thesis is that they grow up with money, are told they are special because they have money, and never need to work a day in their lives and they know it. As a result, they generally consider anyone without money beneath them.

For some reason, I was seen as a particularly prize target for these tossers, especially in those early years. Physical and physiological bullying was a daily treat. I missed my old friends dearly and the safety of those long-term relationships. I knew how to navigate those old waters; I knew my standing. I was lonely with these new people, in this new place. Add to that the father at home I was terrified of, and they were some tough years. Mine was not the family in which you could pour out your soul at the end of a tough school day, cry, get a hug and some kind and wise words. No, mine was more like the "Suck it up and don't be a wimp" family, the "I don't even want to hear it" family.

At school I withdrew, better to be as invisible as possible than to draw more attention from the tribes all around. I would spend lots of time in the library, hidden in the corner reading sci-fi and adventures. One particular kid got his kicks out of physically assaulting me, and there was really no safe way to avoid this. I went to a teacher and asked what would happen if I "finally lose my shit" and beat the living hell out of this kid. The teacher suggested it would probably not go well, but could offer no other useful advice.

As a side note, it still remains a bit of a mystery to me as to when one should be a pacifist, and when one should go "ape shit" and smack the bully upside the head. In my case, I found the middle ground, pushing back, physically, making it clear that I might just be capable of at least inflicting serious injury to said bully even if I might ultimately be defeated. It seemed to work, the bullying became less serious and less often. To this day, I aggressively seek to avoid any confrontation, but bullying drives me crazy and I cannot stand for it.

So, against this backdrop of bullying, loneliness, and lack of a tribe, I got very depressed. Though I did not recognize it then, I even developed what I would now call a fractured psyche. I began to fantasize, which all kids do, but in my case, it morphed from fantasy to something much less benign. I actually began to believe I was a secret superhero with secret powers, including the ability to fly. Again, not a particularly dangerous fantasy, unless the kid is clinically depressed and suicidal. Which, it turns out in retrospect, I was.

On one occasion, I stood on the edge of a very high pillar on the school grounds with a clear, maybe seventy-five-foot drop to the concrete below. On this day, a particularly bad day, I had decided I would show everyone that I could fly. If I could fly, the fractured psyche noted, I would go from loser to hero. Then the next revelation: if I could not fly, I would most certainly die and frankly, that would be an okay outcome as well. As you may have guessed by now, I did not take the plunge (or I can fly and that seems unlikely). I guess, in the end, the unbroken part of my brain knew I could not fly and the deeper, perhaps reptilian part of my brain wanted to live, so I did not take the step. But I never forgot how it felt to consider doing so.

Even now, it is with great heartache that I read about teen suicide and how it has only increased in the last few years. I don't question how these kids ended up in such a terrible place, because I can remember how I got there. I wish I could gather all these kids and tell them it can get better, the dark days can be over, but it is not so simple. Being human is a dangerous affair, we must be very careful to not break each other. There are kids around you right now wondering if they can fly and not so concerned if they cannot even as they take that leap. Look out for them, talk to them, let them know they are seen.

Many average kids have been bullied, as it continues to be a persistent problem in the workplace, online, at home—not just in schools. While we may not have the power to stop bullying from happening, one thing the average person can do is call it out when someone else is taking the hit, or at the very least, not join in. It is to my great shame that I joined in on some of the bullying at school for a time. The fact that it has haunted me for over forty-five years offers a bit of insight: ten minutes of bullying someone to feel part of a tribe is not worth the decades of self-loathing that can come with it. Trust me on this. You don't have to be a superhero to stand up to the bullying of another person. You can just stand up, call "BS," and walk away. If enough average people band together and just do that, the bully loses their audience and that is all that they care about.

Perhaps the greatest thing the average person can be is kind. Kindness, it turns out, can save lives. One act of kindness can outweigh a ton of bullying. It doesn't take a lot of hard work or intelligence to be kind. It just takes a little empathy. It takes remembering how it felt to be bullied or "othered," and that's something all average people have in common. The more average or broken a person is, often the better they are at showing kindness because they can relate. There is extraordinary power in being average, and perhaps the greatest of all powers is to simply be kind.

My Greatest Achievement

ONE OF THE UPSIDES TO having no friends, no social life, and no girls to distract me from working is that I started, for the first time, to do well, really well, at school. The constant drumbeat of my father telling me to go to medical school was being internalized. My father's brother was a doctor, and I always knew my father desperately wanted to be one, and in fact, pretended to be one all of our lives, giving us medications and cures for things he knew nothing about, prescribed with his exceptional egotistical confidence. But it was my brilliant and quite unicornian uncle who changed my life with some kind and encouraging words. My uncle, the "infomanic," threw a life vest to a drowning kid.

Uncle Dave was a physician and one of the most wonderfully eccentric people I have ever met. He was exceptionally bright, able to remember long strings of facts after a single reading. He trained in radiology in Australia and passed the board examinations in Australia, England,

and the United States. In the 1970s, he took the family to the United States and became Professor of Radiology in Pittsburg. He was proudly on the autism spectrum, developing ever increasingly strange social behavior as he got older, which included telling rambling stories with seemingly no point (or at least none the listener could discern), or horrifyingly embarrassing ones to his immediate family. Most memorable to me was the way he seemed to try and capture all the knowledge in the world, no matter how trivial or weird. It made for a chaotic but endlessly interesting house full of books and crazy notebooks.

Uncle Dave was obsessed with books, and bought literally tens of thousands of them from bookstores across the world and later from Amazon. When visiting him in the last years of his life, I noticed Amazon would drop off a series of packages containing three, four, sometimes six or more books, daily, which would then pile up in the cars, house, and garage. He would speed read sections of them, then put them away along with the rest of the enormous and ever-growing library which also included DVD's and VHS tapes. He watched and recorded everything he possibly could: documentaries, science shows, anything that contained information of any kind.

He also took to making scrapbooks of information. Pages of newspapers, books, magazines, often with his writing scribbled in between the margins. Perhaps the best part of this particular habit was that he would tape fifty-dollar bills randomly between the clippings, so no one would throw them away without looking at every page to try and find the loot—though this is now somewhat in dispute in the family. Eccentric, expensive, and kind of genius!

Despite all of this, or perhaps because of it, he had an outsized effect on me. So, when I reached a crisis in high school about what to do with my life, it was him I turned to for advice. His advice was "simple"—go to medical school. It had helped him with all his issues, and it happened to be a very secure job, bringing with it some prestige and self-esteem, so I should do it. Sounded simple. There was just one small problem with this genius idea from this genius man: Uncle Dave was a smart guy with a remarkable memory who was incredibly well read and on the spectrum. I did not have his smarts or his memory, so for me to get into medical school would be an enormous lift. I did have a few things going for me. One, zero social life to distract me, and two, an obsessive-compulsive disorder-like syndrome (though not to the degree my uncle had). When I decided to do something, really do something, I was all in. So, I went all in on study.

At the time, getting into university, medical school, law school, the arts, whatever, was based on a score given in one's final year of high school. The universities created tests for the various subjects and gave one test to rule them all to final-year high school students in the state. For each subject you would get a grade and a numeric score. Count up your score and that was the number that determined what university and what course you could get into. If you applied to medicine, which had the most difficult entrance requirements, your chance of beating out the many tens of thousands of other kids putting "medicine" on the top of their application was statistically close to zero. It was all based on that one score. Simple, terrible, but *simple.*

I am often amazed by my American friends and family when they talk about how much they loved their last year of the "high school" experience. That golden season when they had already secured a university position and were free to plot their futures and enjoy the fading light on their high school lives with all the friends they had made along the way. In Australia, my last year of high school was a pressure-filled, anxiety-ridden hellscape. Never before had I been challenged to practice the dreaded concept of delayed gratification to such an intense degree.

Teachers and counselors had been singing the praises of delayed gratification for as long as I could remember. It went like this: work today and you can play tomorrow. Play today and you will have to work tomorrow, often long after others have "retired." If you want to go to college, a good college, a hard to get into college, you have to forgo some of the pleasures of the now. If you want to save for a new car, you have to not buy every shiny thing you see, you have to delay that gratification. If you go to a party every night, never study, you will have a grand time, but unless you are some kind of genius, you are not going to college. Turns out, for the average person, and certainly the average student like me, delayed gratification must become a part of your makeup, and the good news is that with practice, you can get better at it.

Every day after school I would go to gymnastics and

train with the team, then go home and do at least six hours of study without fail, and much more on weekends. It was relentless. I took practice tests, wrote an essay a night, memorized physics problems, did so many math equations I felt like I could land a man on the moon with a slide rule myself. That stress was felt by everyone I knew; it played out in high schools across the country and came at serious cost to many of us. We developed a form of PTSA. If you wanted to secure the best university and the best degree, it is just what you did.

Then the day(s) come. You go to a vast hall with all your fellow students, pencils in hand, erasers at the ready, vomit everywhere. Okay, not everywhere, but the stress was so high it was not uncommon to see people blowing chunks on the way to and from the exam rooms. You had this very real sense that if you screwed up today, your life was over. Any real chance of happiness and a career was done. You had very clear and simple guidelines: score big or be forever wondering *what if*. You felt you were competing against every other student in the state for a precious few positions. As an average student, trying to achieve beyond my real abilities, this was a tall order.

Despite the odds, you did the tests, then you compared notes, and what a disaster that was. "What did you get for the answer to Physics question number seven? The one about working out the orbital velocity of a kitten thrown out of the space shuttle under full throttle, in the middle of a solar flare, the moment after the aliens had destroyed the moon thus reducing its pull of gravity?" Inevitably, your answer, in meters per second, was nowhere near their answer, in kittens per foot. One of you was wrong. It went this way from one subject to another. Chemical complexes were created that had not been seen in nature or in the lab, but you were sure eight thousand carbon atoms to one helium atom was a real compound. You get the idea.

But the pain didn't stop there. After you finished the exams, you had to wait for weeks, months even, to get the results. You waited patiently by the mailbox—yes, no email, just letters, or perhaps the newspaper where many exam results were published so your humiliation could be complete. Then one fateful day it arrived and . . . your scores were good, but were they good enough? Turns out, I got two A's and 3 B's. There was no way I was getting into the top medical school in the city, but I might have a chance of sneaking into the second one. In Australia, back in the day, it was the overwhelming tradition to apply only to universities in your state. The exams were state specific, and for medical school there were two options: the University of Melbourne, the oldest and by far the most prestigious in the minds of us students, and Monash University, the relatively new and less prestigious upstart. To get into either, however, would be a crowning achievement that any student should and would be proud of.

In late 1982, I got word that the letters of acceptance from the universities had been mailed, and people I knew were getting their acceptance and rejection letters. I still remember going to the mailbox and seeing the letter. I turned it over and did what every normal person would do in the circumstances. I prayed to all the gods in heaven and those not in heaven, promising that I would never do anything wrong again if they could see it in their hearts to have this letter say I made it into medical school. I opened it and, to my great amazement, shock, and mostly enormous gratitude and relief, I saw that I had been accepted to Monash University.

I cannot put into words how much this meant to me. I have received numerous awards in education from local, national, and international bodies, none of which I really deserve. This achievement, however, was the ultimate, because it was mine. This average kid from below average beginnings worked harder than I thought possible and achieved what I thought was pretty much impossible. I have no doubt there was lots of luck involved, too. Lucky because I had a role model in my uncle, lucky even that I had been pushed by an over demanding and terrifying father. I felt lucky then and I feel lucky now. I was in all respects an average kid, who because of hard work and some serious luck, had achieved something extraordinary.

The Hawkeye Model

AT THIS POINT, I FEEL I should be explaining how it was that Sir William Olser, or one of the ancients of the medical crafts, was my inspiration in medicine. Real men and women who once walked the hallowed halls of some long-ago hospital, doing great things for their patients and even greater things for all mankind. But these were not, in fact, my role models. My role model was a comic on an early 1970s TV show I happened to love called *MASH*. Alas, we do not get to choose our inspiration, they choose us, and for me it was Hawkeye.

If you have not seen the TV show *MASH*, do yourself a favor and watch it. Not the movie of the same name, which was good, but the TV series. It followed the exploits of a series of quirky and wonderful fictional characters in a Mobile Army Surgical Hospital (MASH) during the Korean War (though it was actually about the Vietnam war). The main character played magnificently by Alan Alda was Hawkeye Piece, a doctor, a humanist, a technically excellent surgeon, a womanizer, a comic, a man who did not want to be in a war zone. During each episode the team would be faced with terrible decisions, moral dilemmas, and through all of it they made us laugh and think.

For me, and I suspect (from my conversations with them) a generation of physicians, Hawkeye was the doctor we all wanted to be. He was smart, so very good at his craft, he cared deeply about his patients, the entire patient, and loved his team. In the face of all manner of adversity he could crack a joke and lead a team to greatness. He was also handsome—the ladies loved him and the men respected him. I wanted to be that guy! *MASH* ended the year I got into medical school but it is not an exaggeration to say that as I watched it each week, it inspired me to make it to medical school and to eventually *be* that guy.

Later, I would work on a tiny surgical ward in a tiny hospital, with a small team that also fancied themselves in the Hawkeye mold. We would make jokes with the patients and each other and carried on a very non-traditional "rounding" on the patients. The lead surgeon was a wonderful, humble guy everyone loved. The registrar in charge (the lead resident) had a great sense of responsibility and an equally great sense of humor. We "got" each and had a shared humor and fascination with the absurd (as my third-grade teacher called it). One thing these doctors taught me is that patients, in general, love to laugh, like real patients, not just the ones on TV. There is something therapeutic and analgesic about humor and laughter. It is also a great way to break the ice and the sense of dread that surrounds so many people in the hospital, many of whom are rightly wondering if they will ever leave.

When rounding, this team and I would make fun of each other, the politics of the day, and even the diseases we were treating. The lead surgeon was once consenting an elderly woman for a complicated surgical treatment of her cancer when, at the end, she asked what was the worst that could happen. He paused thoughtfully and said, "I guess the worst that can happen is I slip and cut your aorta and you bleed to death. Also, the anesthesiologist could come in drugged and forget to sedate you and you'll remember the entire thing. Also, your insurance could get unexpectedly canceled, and while you'll be dead, your children will have a crushing financial burden for years to come." A pause followed. Then, she burst out laughing and we all followed. "Okay," she said, "let me reword that." Another time, he was telling an elderly man his cancer was terminal and there was nothing he could do, but that we would keep him comfortable and pain-free. He then looked around at all of us then back to the man and said, "The good news is you're not alone. None of us, *none* of us—not even these kids here (pointing at me)—are getting out of this world alive." Again, the pause, then the man said "Damn straight. Make the most of it, docs."

The patients loved that we were having fun and making them part of it, and I think they loved it because they also knew our lead surgeon was excellent. I am not sure how it would have gone if we were having fun and making fun and our leader was incompetent. Perhaps that is a rule: you can break the mold and be light in the face of difficult things, and lead a merry group of professionals, but you had better be good at your job first. In my experience, laughter really can be exceptional medicine. Yes, one has to know the audience, be culturally sensitive, and understand that there is a difference between humor that comes from a place of caring and dark humor that is a substitute for caring. If you don't know the difference, perhaps keep the jokes to yourself.

Hawkeye modeled many of the things I wanted to be, most of all relevant, good, and I guess, if I were honest, some kind of "powerful." If I could make it to medical school, I would, in my thinking, be someone who had achieved something very difficult. The key elements in Hawkeye's character were simple: compassion, passion, and honesty. There were, of course, many other things that made him attractive, but we were drawn to him because of that compassion and passion and the fact that he was real. We cannot all be Hawkeye or Patch Adams but we can be human. We can see the humor in even the worst tragedies. If we take the time to be human, to laugh together, we can be heroes in the moment.

To this day, I love the model Hawkeye set. The average person can learn a lot from his example. Average people, like you and I, can tell our terrible jokes with a clean conscience and a good heart and the patients (or co-workers or team mates) will love it. Average people can be all the things Hawkeye was: kind, compassionate, real, and excellent at their work. Average people can make other people feel seen, respected, even loved. Average people, because they are average, can know what it is like to be seen and therefore see those around them. Average people can surround themselves with like people and, as a team, become so much more than average.

Learning to Be Human

DESPITE THE HUGE RELIEF AND sense of achievement I felt getting into medical school, the supreme effort of it left me spent. Frankly, the first few years after high school I was academically burnt out. All that work, all those hours, I was just crispy burnt out. I passed everything, but that was about it. Many Australian kids take a year off after high school to travel the world and reboot before college. I did not have the courage to do that, I went straight into a seven-year medical school after high school. And then I struggled.

I was not the only one suffering from this burnout. Out of a class of around two hundred, something like fifty people did not make it to the second year. Some decided medicine was not for them, some failed out, some just kind of disappeared. Burnout is a real thing, especially if you have entered a place where everyone is smart and hard-working and you are just trying to keep up. You leave high school at the top of your class, you enter medical school and everyone is at the top of their class and you become, overnight, academically speaking, average yet again. Yes, there are some rare students who are so exceptional they go from exceptional high school students and immediately become exceptional medical students, but they are, you guessed it, the exception that proves the rule.

I loved learning all of the new information, but the effort to really consolidate it, to really know the material, was enormous. It got better over time as we got closer to the clinical content and further away from the base science. Still, I struggled; there is just so much to learn, so many facts and figures and concepts. For an average student, it's a huge stretch. I remember having a really hard time learning basic names in anatomy. I asked my friends about a million times "What is the anatomical name for the collarbone?" At first, they thought it was a joke. Over time, they became seriously concerned I needed a CAT scan because it was clear that my brain didn't work right. That struggle, however, was the clear and overwhelming reason I became a better doctor and an even better teacher. By the way, it's clavicle.

Again, in a scene from one of my favorite movies, *Good Will Hunting,* the protagonist played by Matt Damon is a math genius surrounded by other really bright professors and students. He, however, is a true math genius, his brain is wired for math and he is simply in another league. At a particular moment of frustration with his professor, he proclaims, "Do you know how easy this is for me? Do you have any fucking idea how easy this is?

This is a fucking joke! And I'm sorry you can't do this, I really am, because I wouldn't have to fucking sit here and watch you fumble around and fuck it up." My point: it is truly a rare person who is exceptionally gifted at a thing and also able to relate to the average person when it comes to that thing. On the other hand, those who really struggle with learning a thing relate to other people's struggles. If it takes you hours to memorize some basic facts and you meet someone else having the same issue, it can be a bonding experience. Rather than the frustrated, f-bomb rant of the genius above, they might say to you, "I get it, I understand. I had the same issue, but you got this, because I did it and we are exactly the same." Which, obviously, is way more helpful to the person now in your position.

Not being a particular good student has made me, somewhat paradoxically, a better teacher. I *really* understand those people who struggle with understanding a concept or learning a string of facts. I *really* understand people who cannot remember the name for the collarbone, and can assure them they don't need a CAT scan. If with that understanding comes empathy, then you can be a great teacher. Remember the struggle, the pain, the frustration of not being able to do a thing easily and make it your superpower. I cannot emphasize this point enough: it can be life changing. If you are struggling with that topic, that sport, that relationship, whatever it is, don't ever forget how that struggle felt. Having struggled will make you, if you choose to let it, a great teacher and mentor to all the other average students out there.

I see this in sports as well. Many of the world's best athletes are not the best coaches. And many of the best coaches were good, but not exceptional athletes. I think the great coaches often had to struggle, practice harder, think more, and because of it, be able to relate better to most of the players, who are by definition average. The exceptionally talented players may have a hard time explaining how you hit a forty-foot three-pointer ten times a game—the feel, the release, the timing. To them, most of it happens at an unconscious level. The person who's worked hard to become a great three-point shooter can tell you every single step in the process because they had to learn, unlearn, relearn, try, fail, fail, and try again to develop the skill. The best teachers, coaches, people are often not those who were the best at that pursuit, but that very fact, their very averageness, makes them exceptional teachers and coaches.

After medical school came residency for me. Residency is a period of a number of years where you see patients under the supervision of more senior physicians in an educational environment aimed at taking you from the theory of medicine (medical school) to the practice of medicine. Residencies vary by specialty and by country. In the United States, most medical residencies are three or four years, sometimes as long as seven years for surgical residences. In Australia, residency can easily extend to ten years, as it is a different system than in the US. "Residents" are used as cheap labor so much of the training is more service than actual training.

Residency was a particularly intense time, the hours were long, the learning intense, and the stakes high. If you screwed up a medical school test you got a bad score, you felt bad, but no one died. In residency if you screwed up a patient's care, and the physician in charge didn't catch it, someone could get hurt, people could die. This was—and is—the dirty and terrifying little secret about residency and the practice of medicine. You will make mistakes and sometimes that hurts people. I made my fair share, and I can directly relate mistakes I made to my patients dying before their time. To say this is a tremendous burden is a ridiculous understatement. It's one of the reasons suicide rates, drug and alcohol abuse, and burnout are much higher for physicians than the rest of the community. It is a very stressful job and everyone, *everyone*, makes a mistake at some point. Having made a mistake, one has to then live with that fact the rest of your life. This, again, can be an example of how being average can make you a good mentor.

One of the most terrible things you can do is make a mistake that hurts a patient. The first time it happened to me in residency, I was completely devastated. I had forgotten to follow up a test result, a mistake that resulted in the patient having a cardiac arrest from renal failure. While it is true this patient was quite ill and may have died soon anyway, this was not comforting to me. I went to my professor and told him I couldn't do this, could not be a doctor. I would never get over this. He was a wonderful man, an amazing doctor and the perfect mentor. He made it clear that every doctor goes through this, and it feels terrible, just terrible, but you have to go on. Over your career you will help many more people that you will harm, and you have to be okay with this. The trick is to allow your mistakes to make you better, study more, learn more, be more careful, more anal retentive.

These were fine words presented in a caring and compassionate way, but the thing that really helped was knowing that this incredible physician, a person I so admired for his skill and knowledge, had done the same thing. This guy, this god-like figure, had screwed up as well and a patient had died because of it. It was knowing that fact, that we are all human, we are all in fact average at some point, that got me through. It still upsets me to this day, along with every other mistake I have made. These scars, however, this averageness, would eventually become one of my best attributes as a teacher.

In residency, a colleague once saw a baby who had presented with some minor complaint and was brought in by their parents. After a thorough history and exam and some targeted tests, this resident sent the baby home. The next day, the baby presented in cardiac arrest and ultimately died. Perhaps this resident had omitted one minor step that may have led to the diagnosis and may have resulted in a different outcome, perhaps they had not. This person had done nothing wrong, but medicine and life can be cruel, and it was the end of a career before it had begun. Although this was a smart and lovely physician, beloved by the patients, nurses and other doctors, this terrible incident made them leave the practice of medicine.

I have counseled many residents in my life, many times about mistakes they have made or the sad and tragic cases that just happen. I have told them to forgive themselves, that being human is an imperfect thing. But it's only when I tell them that I have done the same that they can really hear that call to self-forgiveness. I tell them of my colleague who left medicine and what a great loss that was for our profession and their potential patients. How many people would have been saved and comforted and had better lives had they stayed. That doctor would have been able to relate to the worst stories, the saddest clinicians, the most demoralized of physicians, and would have made them feel so much better.

Being average, suffering a great tragedy, can be a kind of terrible gift, a gift no one wants, but a gift to someone else just the same. If you have made a mistake, if you could have done better, if life handed you a tragedy, if you are strong enough to survive it, you, too, can be the wounded healer. We need you to come alongside us, help us forgive ourselves, remind us what it is to be human, to be average.

The "Smart" Doctor

AFTER MEDICAL SCHOOL, I BECAME a clinical teacher, an academic, a professor in one of those residencies I talked about. I was an okay doctor, better than some, not as good as others. There are a lot of smart people in medicine so being average feels pretty good. I would call myself a better than average educator precisely because I was *not* a great student. That fact, that struggle, meant I could relate to all of the medical and nursing students, residents, and junior doctors as they started their life in medicine. Many people who had made it this far in the profession were just like me, average students with above average motivation and an ability to defer gratification, who now found themselves surrounded by people they were pretty sure were way smarter than them. In fact, they were not.

In medicine, the idea of being smart is very much sought after. Smart in this case does not actually mean an IQ of two hundred. In medicine, smart refers to someone with a huge knowledge base who can use it when seeing patients. Someone who can read a textbook about an obscure disease, remember it, and recognize it in a patient they see years later. Smart is someone who has seen thousands of people with appendicitis and now has a unique understanding of the disease, in all the ways it can present, and because of that, they get fooled less than the average doctor. Smart is someone who seems to have read every single medical article on a topic, impossible as that may be.

It turns out, even the average medical student can become a really "smart" physician by these standards. The first step is understanding that all of these really smart doctors are not, in most cases, smarter than you, but that they have worked hard and . . . smart. The smart doctor does this during their training and for the rest of their career, and I suspect this is true in every single job. The smart doctor stops worrying about how inadequate they feel or, to put it another way, turns their anxiety about feeling inadequate into a series of actions to make them feel less inadequate.

In medicine, the feeling of being an imposter is extremely common; the feeling is pretty much ubiquitous. In fact, I would say if you don't feel like an imposter at least some of the time, you are probably pretty dangerous. Arrogance in medicine definitely comes before the fall. Medicine is so complex, there are so many diseases, so much complex physiology that varies from person to person. Diseases present in so many different and subtle ways that it is just a matter of time before you get bit on the buttocks. One minute you can feel like a genius, the next like a fool. Let me tell you an example from my own career.

Perhaps you have heard of the dreaded "flesh eating bacteria." Sounds terrifying because it is, and it is quite real. It seems the lay press picks up on this every few years because it is the kind of thing to keep you up at night. In general terms, there are two types of this disease, one occurring in patients who are old, or immunosuppressed, who suffer from diabetes or alcoholism or often some combination of all of them. These patients are at very high risk of lots of different infections and "flesh eating bacteria" is one of them. The other kind is a particularly terrible bacteria, one of the streptococcus species in particular, that can infect and kill even young and otherwise apparently healthy people. Most streptococcus species are not so bad, a sore throat, a little fever, better in a week or so. Not so with some strains that can literally invade and destroy healthy tissue and kill you fast. In either case, the bacteria can infect the deeper layers of the skin and digest those layers and spread incredibly quickly. If the infection is not literally cut out, the patient can die within days.

The problem is this infection can be hard to diagnose and, initially, can look like other much more common, much less severe, skin infections. In a one-week stretch in a hospital where I worked, I saw four such cases. The first was obvious: the patient was very ill, had a high fever, a fast heart rate, and gas in their tissues on X-ray. Off to the operating room and the diagnosis was confirmed and the patient saved. The next patient presented with an infection on the face that looked particularly bad and, as it turned out, her husband was in our ICU with "flesh eating bacteria." She had the area removed, the diagnosis confirmed, and she did well. The third patient was a young healthy woman in her early twenties with what looked like a skin infection on her arm, but something about her made us a little more concerned. She was just a little sicker than the average person and we wondered why she, a healthy person, had gotten his infection without any trauma or scratch that she could remember.

We asked the surgeons to come and take a look but they were not impressed and said with confidence that it was just a routine infection. However, the longer she stayed in our ER the more convinced we were she had the disease. Her pulse kept going up, her pain was hard to control, and she just didn't look good. We called the surgeons back to see her and they again said there was nothing for them to do, it was a standard infection. We disagreed and asked (demanded) that the senior surgeon come and see the patient. He did and, while not completely convinced, he took her to the operating room and, to his horror, the diagnosis was confirmed and she had to have extensive removal of skin and muscle from her arm, almost dying in the process.

The next day the surgeons came down and told us all how "smart" we were and, let me tell you, this never happens! Since I was the doctor in charge and got most of the praise, I was feeling particularly good about myself and my skills as a physician. The very next day a very "smart" resident came on shift and asked what I was doing with the patient in bed number four with necrotizing fasciitis (flesh eating bacteria). I assured him that patient had a large blood clot in his leg and was awaiting an ultrasound to confirm the diagnosis. He disagreed and we went to see the patient together. To my horror, the diagnosis of necrotizing fasciitis was obvious and I had straight up missed it. Just days after being told how smart I was, here I was, fooled by an obvious case my resident had to point out to me. The patient went to the operating room, had extensive skin and muscle removed, and survived but with a very long hospital course. One moment in medicine you can look like a legend, the next, a fool.

Maximum humility is required in this, as in many jobs. Medicine can bite you in the buttocks just when you are absolutely sure you know what is going on. Being careful is more important than being smart. I learned to reexamine and reexamine and check and check again any patient who was more than a little sick. Disease changes over time and we need to be on the lookout. It is why "smart" doctors will tell you, "I think you have X and we should do Y, but if things change, please come back so we can check you again." I also found that my misses and near misses have been the best motivator to get "smarter." After this series of cases, I read everything I could about the disorder and all the ways it could present. I talked to colleagues, shared my story, listened to theirs, and got as smart as I could about this very serious condition.

Experiences like this made me want to be a teacher. Turns out, one of the best remedies for feeling like a fraud is to become as expert at something as possible, while always remembering there is more to learn. And one of the best ways to become expert at something is to be able to teach it. In order to teach it, you have to understand it, read all about it, and collect your thoughts into a logical sequence. The best defense against a future screw up, in medicine or whatever job you do, is to make every mistake a teaching moment for yourself, and for anyone who might benefit from the knowledge. If you are average, you can learn from your own mistakes and from those around you, and in the process, make yourself much more than average, maybe even smart.

As you can imagine, my students liked to hear these stories of me making mistakes, really screwing up. It made them feel less inadequate, they could relate, it made them feel better knowing that the professor had made mistakes just like them. It created an environment where we didn't have to try and be perfect, we simply had to try and be better. A little better every time, a little "smarter" every day, then over the months and years, we all can be smart. *Very* smart, if mixed with a big ole helping of humility. I suspect this is true in every job, profession and probably all parts of life. Doctors are no different from the person who cuts the grass, we all have room to grow, become smarter. Being average doesn't mean you have to stay average. Being average, learning from our mistakes and those of others, can mean, over time, we might even become extraordinary.

A Little Imposter Syndrome Goes a Long Way

WEBSTER DICTIONARY DEFINES IMPOSTER SYN-DROME as, "The persistent inability to believe that one's success is deserved or has been legitimately achieved as a result of one's own efforts or skills."

It is my observation that the average person, doing anything much more than getting off the couch, will feel some version of imposter syndrome. As I mentioned in the previous chapter, it's common in medicine and I have seen it in every single honest physician I have ever met. In fact, every single person of integrity I have ever met.

For me, it looks something like this: I am standing in front of a crowded room giving a talk on something I have spent years studying and writing about and researching, but feeling very inadequate. In my head is a voice saying, *Who am I to be standing in front of these people? There are tons of people here smarter, more insightful, and with more experience than me, I should sit the hell down and shut the hell up!* It also happens at the bedside, looking after patients, assuring them that their child will be fine, but in my head thinking, *Am I right? This is a big decision. What if I'm wrong, will this child be harmed? Who the hell do I think I am making such decisions? I'm a complete and utter fraud!* Sure, I studied for years, saw thousands of patients, talked to colleges about the diseases I treated, spent thousands of hours on continuing education. But, hell, I'm just one person at the end of the day. People don't know my weaknesses, the insecurities I carry, the prior mistakes I've made. Most doctors, at various moments in their career, think people must be out of their minds listening to anything we have to tell them.

After getting into medical school, I walked around on cloud nine for a long time, proud and amazed that I had actually accomplished this. People around me were also extremely complementary and proud. In our extended family, I was the talk of the town: Mel, our Mel, our very average Mel had made it to Medical School! I think there was a shared sense that if I could do this, then they could do something extraordinary too, since we shared 99.5% of our genes. I was learning a lot, every day presented a bunch of new facts and ideas, and while it was early, I could see I was on the way to becoming a doctor.

The thing about being a medical student is that people start treating you like a doctor well before they should. And you start thinking you are one, and are happy to take their questions and render your not-at-all-learned opinion. But sometimes, something happens that in an instant makes you realize you don't know jack. You realize that you are, in fact, an imposter. You are no doctor, you are a total fake, and soon everyone is going to find out and all those pats on the back will be replaced by sideways looks and eye rolls. In my case, it was a crash that revealed my imposter status.

Late one night in my first or second year of school, I was home alone and heard a terrifying crash outside. I ran out the front door to see what had happened, and right in front of our house a car had smashed into a parked car. To my horror, there was a man in the driver's seat, slumped over and bleeding, breathing irregularly and clearly dying. There I was, the proud medical student, all this new knowledge, all these people patting me on the back, me patting myself on the back, and at that moment I knew exactly zero about what to do. This man was about to die in front of me and I was useless to him. A complete and utter imposter.

While I stood there stunned into paralysis, another car pulled up and a guy jumped out. He assessed the scene and reached into the damaged car and did something I thought miraculous, which turned out to be a fairly basic airway repositioning maneuver. The driver was extremely intoxicated and had impaled his neck against the steering wheel. Once the guy repositioned the victim, immediately his breathing slowed and I was instructed to call 911. Turns out, that random guy was a medical resident currently working in the local Emergency Department. He was on his way home from a shift when he saw the accident occur and came to see if everyone was okay. I don't know the probabilities of that kind of coincidence, but I have no doubt he saved that man's life, and that I was no good to him.

Imposter syndrome is powerful. Those feeling of shame and sadness at being an imposter changed my life. I felt terrible, guilty, useless, like a complete fake. That incident, and a few more like it, made me decide I needed to learn how to deal with streetside emergencies, whether they were trauma incidents, heart attacks, stroke, bleeding, babies being delivered in the back of cars—I was going to do Emergency Medicine and learn to be a "real doctor." That event, followed by my imposter syndrome, sent me on the long road to training in Emergency Medicine in two countries and starting an education program for Emergency Medicine used the world over. That incident was the start, decades later, of a nonprofit that today works in over 150 countries accelerating Emergency Medicine education.

I believe this imposter syndrome is ubiquitous in every thoughtful person doing difficult things with big risks—perhaps because it is a sign of humility. We see the expert standing up there giving a great talk, having such well-crafted ideas, thoughts, and presentations and assume they know what they are talking about. I can tell you there is a very good chance that that speaker is stressed and wondering why they are putting themselves out there like this *and* thinking they are an imposter. I cannot tell you how many world experts I know in medicine, especially in the field of Emergency Medicine, who in private tell me that when they give public talks they feel like a fraud. When they disclose this, my response now is always the same: "Good, that means you're in exactly the right place."

A true expert on a topic understands what they do not know. They understand that no one can know everything and recognize the limitations of being a person. Becoming an expert at something doesn't stop you from being human, doesn't somehow give you the superpower of being all-knowing and all-insightful. In fact, the speaker that gets up there and does not have imposter syndrome is much more likely to have a personality disorder than the one who has it. A real expert thinks, "I have so much more to learn." It can feel like importer syndrome, and yet it is exactly the right state of mind. The really great thinkers and speakers let the crowd know this without false humility. They don't say, "I'm really not that smart and I don't know much, but here's my talk." They say something like, "I've thought about this topic a lot, read as much as I can, talked to as many experts as I can, and here are my current insights. Let me share them, and then I'd like to hear your thoughts, because I bet there are people in this audience who have seen this disease more times than me and have their own insights." This is the humble expert; one I can now relate to and one for whom the imposter syndrome is having an appropriate effect on the ego.

When I speak to people in other fields, the experts in all manner of things at a level I cannot imagine, from music to science to lawn care, I hear the same thing. Imposter syndrome is extremely common, it can feel uncomfortable, but the very feeling of the "syndrome" is a healthy thing. The unease of it can be the key to getting better at that thing. If we feel inadequate, then this can be the furnace that makes us want to learn more. As long as it doesn't become pathological, it is a real driver of continued innovation and education. Not only is imposter syndrome perfectly acceptable, I dare suggest it is important, really important, to anyone trying to master difficult things. Having imposter syndrome doesn't make you average, it simply means you are exactly, perfectly normal. Accept the universal nature of the disorder and make it the engine for your own worthy self-improvement. When you do this, all those around you win. Imposter syndrome can make the average anything but average over time.

Even Experts Make Mistakes

AFTER RESIDENCY, I BEGAN MY career in academic medicine and as part of that, started speaking on the "tour"—which involved teaching at the residency, then teaching in local hospitals and later at national and international conferences. I had some natural talent for this but the standard was high. At my residency was perhaps the most famous physician in our specialty and a master at speaking and lecturing. He could weave stories into the medical literature that kept us all on the edge of our seats, with profound insights and an excellent ability to convey them. Compared to his speaking prowess, I knew I was about as average as it gets. His advice on how to get invited to the most prestigious conferences of the day was simple: "Just do a good job." Sounded like a good idea, but what exactly did that mean? He gave me some pointers, to which I've added my own over the years. The key is understanding that any room is, by definition, full of other average people.

One of the best ways I've found to connect with an audience is to let them know you're an ordinary person, just like them. Talk about your mistakes, reveal your weaknesses. Standing in front of an audience talking about a particular topic makes you, by default, some kind of an expert. The expert standing up there and saying, "Here's how I've screwed it up," has a number of effects. One, it bonds the crowd to you; a little honesty and humility go a long way. In the audience, there are always people who have made the same mistake. Having the person with the microphone say they have made that error can make them feel so much better. It is a hard thing to do at first. To admit to colleagues your mistakes, your limitations, is very difficult. Once you do it, and are genuine and open, I guarantee you at the end of your talk people will come up and thank you for it. We are all average, we have all made mistakes. Knowing that the "experts" have, and still are, making mistakes is a whole lot of therapy for a whole lot of people.

Self-deprecating humor is also a big winner. Especially these days when it is possible to upset just about any group, it is better to aim any humor at yourself. I have always thought it safe and fun to make fun of myself and my mistakes. It shows people I don't take myself too seriously. It makes me less likely to get into trouble. Early on in my career, I made a joke about Catholics, having been brought up Catholic I thought it was safe. It was not. After that mistake and many more like them, I realized the best person to make fun of was myself. Not any group I could be associated with, not any tribal feature, just me and me alone.

I have also noticed this idea of humility and self-deprecation has become a popular thing among speakers in recent years, but it can come off as disingenuous and the crowd can see it. If someone gets up and says, "I really don't know much about this topic," then reveals they know pretty much everything about it, that opening salvo has been wasted and had the opposite effect. Claiming to not be very smart, when you clearly are exceptionally well-read and practiced, has the opposite effect than planned. Talking about mistakes and things you have done wrong should come from an honest place—we have all made mistakes, the next thing is just to be honest about it. It is both liberating and exciting when you can reveal your weaknesses and flaws, knowing you are not alone.

I got to watch and be mentored by the best. From my humble genius professor in medical school to the colleagues and friends who were really exceptional, but were also open to revealing to their students and colleagues their mistakes and insecurities. This is a new thing in medicine. For decades, millennia I suspect, doctors have projected confidence, arrogance and a lack of humility, especially with their students. The distance between professor and student was made to seem as wide as possible. The professor knew everything and you, the student, were made to feel like the lessor. Indeed, in some specialties, this was done very aggressively. Students were systematically terrorized by the faculty. In some sick way, the professors thought this was good for them. Embarrassing students was a sport, the worse you made them feel the better you were at the game.

I was in the operating room once with a professor, a surgeon, and I stood at the patient's head working with the anesthesiologist. Another student was working with the vascular surgeon. The patient had a large clot in one of the large arteries in their leg that needed to be removed before the damage to the leg was complete. The way the surgeon did this was to open the skin and artery and place a catheter into the vessel and literally pull out the clot that was under pressure. Often when you do this, there is a brisk squirt of blood just like unclogging any drain under pressure. The surgeon asked the student to stand in a very specific place, then removed the clot and the student was hit with the pulsating, spurting blood, to the great enjoyment of the surgeon and the terror of the student.

I can tell you that today that would never happen. While the old doctors complain about the rules around work hours and protecting students from abuse, a "woke" mindset, this is why these rules are in place. Medicine was once a toxic, misogynistic dumpster fire and the "good old days" were in no way good. Indeed, the pendulum can swing too far and the attempts at protecting students from the stress and long hours of training might go too far, but it is better that the pendulum be allowed to swing and ultimately find the right place to rest, than to not let it swing at all. I find today's professors are a different breed than when I was a student. More of them care about the students, really try and build them up. Remind them that they, too, were once students and the student will one day be the professor.

I have always had the great revelation that the only reason I was the teacher and they were the students is that

I was older than them. It was birth order and not some magical ability that had me currently "outranking" them. This wasn't too far a stretch, as many students who were training at the same time I was were far more advanced than me. And the colleagues that once were my students have gone on to far surpass me in clinical skills and teaching ability.

This is the never-ending cycle we should all be aiming for, whatever our sphere of influence or field of work. Make the student, child, colleague, whoever, better than you so that they can make those who come next better than them. If we do this, then that group will get better over time and we all benefit from the virtuous cycle. With each generation the average should become better; the average should become, over time, much better than average.

Average Stories, Extraordinary Lessons

ONE OF THE BIGGEST PROBLEMS with not understanding that most of us are average is underestimating just how often the average person needs to hear, or learn, or read and reread something to get it into their long-term memory. With this in mind, I wanted to create an educational program that could potentially reach more doctors than I could speaking on tour. At this point in my education endeavors, my best critic, biggest supporter, and closest partner was my wife, Mary. We had met at UCLA when I had taken a year off from medical school to do a research degree in the US. It was a whirlwind romance and, at the end of the year, my visa was about to expire, so it was either get married, or break up and go back to Australia. We got hitched at the ripe age of twenty-three. Crazy idea when I look back, but after thirty-five wonderful years it has worked out pretty great. We shared a passion for education and philanthropy and, together with a mentor of mine, had an idea for a program that would go on to succeed beyond anything we could have imagined.

The idea involved recording audio, then editing it and distributing it via CD and cassette tape each month, plus a little internet offering. Some programs like this were already in existence but we wanted to do it better, more interesting, more fun, using some of the principles outlined about speaking to the "average doctor." Speaking clearly, summarizing and re-summarizing the material was, in part, the special sauce of this program. We told people the information, told them again, then again, and later again, making it fun and interesting in a way that medical education had not been in the past.

Medicine is a very conservative field; the idea of having some fun while learning potentially life-saving information was absolutely foreign. Our insight was that we could actually enhance the learning and even the desire to learn by giving it some personality. Speaking plainly to our subscribers, repeating information, adding jokes, word association and puns was all part of it. Over time, we stepped up our game as we grew and added "sound design." We hired excellent audio engineers and artists to take our audio and add special effects, sounds, parodies, to create something that had not existed in the field of medical education before.

A typical program would start with an introduction and some banter among the physicians about the patients they had seen, the struggles they had, or funny incidents that had occurred. That would set up what we were covering for the month, and then we would ask some target questions that would start the brain moving, get it prepped for what was coming. For example, "Do you know how to treat appendicitis, really? Are you sure? A new study says everything we thought about how to treat it might be wrong!" This gets the clinician's attention. Everyone knows appendicitis is pretty simple to treat: the patient goes to the operating room and have the appendix taken out. Turns out, some recent studies have suggested that for a lot of people this is not needed, at least not initially, and I cannot tell what a major shift in thinking this has been for clinicians. So, you get them thinking but you don't get to the juicy part straight off, leave them hanging and ready to learn.

Later in the program, we might do a piece on how to care for a car accident victim, if you come upon an accident in the street. We, collectively as clinicians, have had this happen many times and it is really easy to screw it up. We would add dramatic music and sound effects of car wheels scratching and cars crashing to add to the mood, the anxiety, to try and reproduce the moment. One of these tragic events, as told on our program, happened to me, and it's another example of how being average can make you more than average.

My wife (a nurse practitioner) and I had come back from a charity event for Homeboy Industries (incredible organization, check them out). We were nicely tucked in bed, sleeping, when, at around three a.m., we heard a crash, at first thinking maybe something had fallen off a truck. A few seconds later, however, we heard screaming, the kind you don't forget, the kind that tells you, immediately, and without any confusion, something truly terrible has happened. We grabbed our shoes, some clothes, and ran out the door. A few houses down from ours, on the street, a car had flipped onto its roof, wheel torn off, gasoline everywhere. A man was screaming that he had "killed his girlfriend." Lying beside the car was a young woman, probably in her early twenties, deeply unconscious.

A few people had gathered, using their phones as flash lights. I ran to the car to see if anyone else was inside, then back to the girl to do a rapid assessment. My wife made sure 911 had been called and was then in the process of crisis intervention. She determined that the man screaming was the driver, he was drunk, there had been a fight, he sped down the road, lost control and flipped the car. His girlfriend had been ejected from the car. He was convinced she was dead and he would go to prison and was about to flee the scene. My wife managed to calm him somewhat and explain that running would only make things worse, then convinced him to sit and wait for the police and ambulance.

While this was happening, I went to the young lady. Her injuries were severe. She had a skull fracture that was depressed, she was unconscious but breathing, she had a dislocated hip and I suspected a serious traumatic brain injury. I carefully positioned her head so she could breathe without moving her neck, as a neck injury is also frequently encountered with these terrible tragedies. I held her head steady and did a maneuver that allowed her airway to open so she could breathe, though it was shallow. What felt like a million years later, the ambulance and police arrived and, after we gave them the information, they gathered the patients and took them away to the local trauma center.

We tell this story on the program for one very simple and basic reason: I screwed up big time. I made fundamental mistakes that could have cost me and others their lives—a lesson that needed to be learned by as many people as possible. It's called *scene safety* and it is paramedic practice 101, but I was a doctor and not trained in scene safety. I had run first to the car, then to the victim, and not once thought about the scene safety. The key first step in a situation like this is make sure you don't make more victims. It was a public street, with cars driving up and down, and I needed to secure the scene so someone didn't add to the mayhem and crash into the people and cars at the site. The idea is to make sure that those trying to help are safe. It was a huge error, and it was only luck that more people, including myself, were not harmed. The average doctor probably would have made the same mistake, so it represented an important teachable moment for many people.

This is the power of average: my mistake was used to tell a true-life story that has no doubt changed the way thousands of clinicians have acted in similar situations. I know this because over the years they have told me they remember that story vividly, and when they found themselves in the same situation thought *scene safety first*. Imagine that, my averageness was turned into another teachable moment. The other effect of telling this story, of course, is therapy. I could, and sometimes do, go over this situation in my mind and get down on myself for being so wrong and reckless. Sharing it, teaching it, and seeing the effect that has had on others has been my therapy. I can revisit it now without so much self-loathing and think, *My mistake helped a lot of people*, and for that I am happy to be average.

Let me share another example of a simple but important lesson the average doctor can learn from. Some dear friends of ours stayed with us over a nearly two-year period while their two boys got bone marrow transplants at the local university hospital. (It's a long story, remarkable and beautifully told by my friend Juli McGown Boit in her book, *From Beyond the Skies*.) Juli is white, Titus, her husband, is Black and Kenyan, and the two boys are Black. My wife and I (both white) helped take the boys on literally hundreds of trips to the hospital and ER for their lifesaving therapy. When the doctors and nurses walked into the room, there could be any number of combinations of adults present, and many of these fine clinicians were instantly confused. *Is this a biracial couple? Whose kids are these?* In almost every case, no one asked the simple question, "How are you related?" Like it was some kind of taboo thing, or they should be able to work it out, or asking was politically incorrect. I have done the same thing too many times to count—assumed relationships that were not, all manner of miscommunication, comic and embarrassing to the extreme.

Average people, even doctors and nurses, cannot walk into a room and work out the genetic or social ties of the people in a room without asking. Here is the big teaching point: just ask. I know it's pretty radical. Just ask, learn the skill. "Hi my name is X, I do Y. Can you tell me your names and how you are all related to each other?" Boom. Confusion avoided, embarrassment averted. All because of a simple question even average people like me can learn to ask. Also, bonus points, never assume a younger woman with a slight bulge in the lower abdomen is pregnant. I have done this and I have watched countless friends and colleagues do it. Learn from our mistakes. The proverb (origin unclear) is correct as proverbs so often are, and it goes something like this: "When we assume we make an ass out of you and me."

The wonderful thing is that this is a simple rule the average person can follow, it takes no genius, indeed it makes life easier. Sometimes it feels like you have to be Sherlock Holmes in social settings but if you just ask, no Sherlocking is required.

The power of being average, so delicious!

The Team Player and
The Narcissist

IN OUR EDUCATIONAL WORK, WE surround ourselves with what I like to think of as genius-average people. Educators who, at the end of a spectacular talk, turn to a colleague and genuinely ask, "What could I have done better? Did this part make sense? Did this illustration work? You know this better than me, was that accurate?" Our production people, after shooting a near perfect scene, will follow with a question to the whole team: "How could we do that better, make it cleaner, shine brighter, sound better?" This team of average people, with this remarkable feedback, insight and humility, becomes extraordinary. Turns out, no matter how smart one person is they cannot match a group of people who are willing to be critiqued and honestly reviewed. A group of average people will make a project as good as it can be, without sucking up all of the oxygen in the room for themselves. A team of ordinarily average people can do extraordinary things.

It has been said if you meet a self-made man, you just meet a liar, or words to that effect. The average person has a keen understanding that if they have had success then they have stood on the shoulders, held the hands of, and generally been dragged there by others. By contrast, the narcissist believes they did it all themselves, that they alone could do it, that without them the thing, whatever it may be, would collapse. The narcissist knows, however, deep down in the places they try and never visit, that they are nothing but average and often less than average. To bolster that fragile psyche, they are quick to point out how smart they are, what great ideas they had that lead to their success. The smart ones will even try to couch it in false humility: "Sure, these other people helped, but in the end, I have this great insight that made it all happen."

It is actually very much like a disease which, if not controlled, becomes more and more toxic over time. The narcissist, if surrounded by other people with actual talent and skill, becomes increasingly insecure. Their defense is to put down anyone perceived as smarter or more successful, to evaluate themselves ever higher. Nothing is ever their fault. And you will never be enough for the narcissist. In fact, if you are too good, you will be the object of their attacks. They will, sometimes in public, often behind the scenes, make sure everyone understands *you* are the problem. First in subtle ways, then, near the end of the relationship, almost always with the ultimate put down, something to the effect of, "You would be nothing without me."

The average achiever sees things very differently. They often cannot believe their success, or feel uncomfortable receiving recognition for what has been achieved, saying things like, "No, no, this was a team sport. I'm just the leader but it took a village." This is not false humility, this is their recognition that in the life of a successful person there is much luck, timing and help. These are people who love to see the team succeed, who revel in the work and the group, and are happy to contribute, knowing that "All ships rise on the tide." They do this with praise and humility, by showing support and letting others take the lead, and by protecting the mistakes or missteps of the rest of the team. Just as they spread the wealth of pride when things go well, they will take the bullets when things go bad.

We have the remarkable luck of working with a tech team made up of wonderful average people that do extraordinary things. One of these team members exemplifies the spectacular attitude of the average overachiever. Often, in our aim to be innovative and try new things, we will want a new feature, a new button, a new way of presenting our materials, which can pose an enormous technical challenge, especially because there is no road map. This particular programmer, when asked to do something difficult and new, will often just smile. A big, beautiful, cat-like grin. What you expect that smile to say is: "I know exactly how to do that, and you're going to think I'm pretty damn smart, and that's going to make me feel pretty damn good!" But it is the exact opposite. That smile, that joy, that glow of a facial expression is followed with, "I have no idea how to do that, but I'll try!" Is that not extraordinary? The joy of seeing a problem, not having any idea how to tackle it, and instead of being withdrawn, angry or passive, they're excited to try and see what happens. People like this are radical, amazing, remarkable, and a joy to work with. There is no pretense about how smart they are, no defenses, they understand their capabilities. They don't have to pretend to be a genius, they can just "try shit out" and if it fails, OK. If it works, wonderful.

Once you are comfortable with the idea that you are average, you can drop the pretense and just try. Once you try, you will find you can do extraordinary things. Once you get rid of the baggage of trying to impress, trying to be something you are not, wonderful things can happen. It takes the right environment, a group of like-minded, wonderful, average people willing to be their average selves together and enjoy the process together. Of course, the average person has emotions and an ego and need to hear "good job" like anyone else but, unlike the narcissist, they are not trying to be seen as superhuman. On a team full of average people where the compliments are genuine and honest and reserved for everyone working for a common goal, the results are exceptional.

I have worked in a number of countries, on many teams and in many departments, and what I've observed is a lot of really smart people but only a few exceptional teams. Too often, too many of these smart people believe they are the key, they are the wonder kid. Listening to them can be comical, usually involving false humility about how they made some incredibly difficult diagnosis. Without saying it directly, they scream, "Look world!

Look at how smart I am!" This will be followed by a similar person telling their story, a little bigger, a little better, a little more difficult patient diagnosis, the teller a little smarter, therefore, than the one before. In no time, this can become a real-world Monty Python sketch featuring grown adults with MDs and PhDs trying to outdo each other. Sadly, the only self-worth they have lies in believing they are the smartest person in the room.

To be sure, in medicine this great desire to be seen as "smart" and to tell the world you are smart, is a disease. We want to be seen as the kings of our domain. Not by bedding the best looking human or slaying the biggest beast, but by making the diagnosis or giving the therapy no one else did. In order to do this, we need to compare. "I saw this patient today sent in by another doctor, they thought they had pneumonia, but I diagnosed them with a pulmonary embolism, the correct diagnosis." Comparing yourself against another in your field and showing yourself to be superior is a daily, even hourly, occurrence in medicine. The inpatient physicians make fun of the lowly ER docs for admitting patients with the wrong diagnosis that *they* got right. The surgeons make fun of the internists for not putting in that difficult IV line or some other procedure that, for them, is mere child's play. On and on it goes. If you were a fly on the wall, you would think medicine is full of the most insecure people on the planet.

This behavior doesn't come from the nastiest place, mostly, it comes from the opposite: a deeply felt sense that you are inadequate. Any time you can compare and show you did a little better than a colleague, you hold onto it. "Look, I'm not completely incompetent." As one matures, you tell less of these stories and start to see the actual truth. The patient with the disease you saw today looked different yesterday; that doctor didn't make the right diagnosis a day ago because neither would you have. Of course, the surgeon can do more and better invasive procedures than the pediatrician, that is their training. Can the surgeon tell the difference between a sick neonate and a not-so-sick child with a fever? Nope, but the average pediatrician can do it in their sleep. This tendency to compare is not just in medicine, it is in all walks of life. I have seen it in farmers, drivers, mechanics, school teachers, lawyers, finance people, and on it goes.

Over time, you stop comparing because you don't need to. You accept you are average and, with the help of all those average people around you, you will get better and, as a whole, make up a team that is not at all average, but extraordinary. When we learn to be happy with our particular skills, without needing to one-up the other, we become much safer, friendlier people. The team player knows what the narcissist either has yet to learn, or refuses to believe: that when we accept ourselves as average, together, we can move a little beyond the average and do the extraordinary.

Game Knows Game

THERE IS A SAYING OR thought in sports that great athletes can pick out other great athletes fast, instinctively. It's something in the moves, the timing, even the way a person carries themselves: *Game knows game.* I am excellent at basketball, piano, lumber cutting, public speaking, and door hanging, and whenever I see someone do what I do, within minutes, I can tell you if they have "game." Like a great coach or a great scout, just doing the thing, practicing the thing, being expert at the thing allows you to recognize an expert in the same area. Now, stay with me here. I'd like to take this a step further and suggest that *good average knows good average.* Let me explain.

Each year, a new set of medical students applies to residency. Before doing so, they often rotate through the departments they would like to join: Pediatrics at Harvard, Surgery at Stanford, Emergency Medicine at UCLA, Family Medicine at a tiny rural medical hospital. Residency directors and their team's job is to work out which of the hundreds of students will be a good fit for their residency. Of course, all of these directors believe, or should believe, that their residency training is the best, or at least exceptional, and they only want exceptional students in their programs. But the best residency directors understand the concept that most doctors, like most people, are, you guessed it, average. What you are looking for is the *good* average. Most students know enough to be good doctors, to be taught the next level of information. Good average (I hearby coin the term) students could be defined as those who care, want to be taught, and are nice people who want the best for their fellow sapiens.

I always used to joke, "Bring me your average and enthusiastic, and we will make them exceptional physicians!" That's because, over time, I was less and less impressed with where a student went to college or medical school. The greatest Harvard graduate who thinks they are the greatest Harvard graduate and therefore cannot be taught, will be a disaster. What does *not* make excellence is "exceptional with attitude." Remarkably smart students from the best schools, if they have an attitude because they have always been the best and have gone to the best schools, can have a hard time imagining anyone not from an equally "good" school being able to teach them anything.

An average student from an average medical school, but one with a big heart, a desire to learn, a real desire to care for their patients, can and will become an exceptional physician. The knowledge base might take a little longer to learn, the initial scores on a variety of tests might be a little lower, but average is good, and good average makes excellent (copyright stamp please).

The average student from the average school with a desire to help and learn will be far more exceptional than the arrogant exceptional student from an exceptional school that already believes they know everything. Again, I say, bring me your average and enthusiastic and we will make them exceptional!

I have no doubt this is true in every field. Take this scenario: Two people apply for your apprentice mechanic position. Both have been working on cars their whole lives, reading lots of articles on the topic, and watching every YouTube video they can get their eyeballs on. One is of average intelligence but is super eager to learn more and is easygoing because of it. The other is exceptionally intelligent and has a remarkable knowledge base, but is also pretty sure they are the smartest person in the room, any room, when it comes to cars. Which student should you take as your apprentice? Go with the average and you can make them exceptional.

The average apprentice with a lust to learn and be part of the team will become, over time, exceptional and loved by their colleagues and customers. The "gunner," unless they change their ways, will always wonder why people are not so fond of them despite the fact they are so damn smart. They will also learn, if they have insight, that in fact, they are nowhere near as smart as they think they are. Worst of all, because their internal and external dialogue is predicated on them being smart, they will have a difficult time admitting mistakes and spend a lot of time blaming others. No one wants to work with that person for too long.

Let's take another example. It's real, but the names and places have been changed to protect the excellent. We had a student come to us from an average medical school with average scores who, initially, wasn't being considered for our prestigious residency. But somehow, she got a rotation for one month in the department and, after that, was at the top of our list. How did this happen? Within just a few days of coming to the department, a place this student did not know, surrounded by people, nurses, doctors, staff she had never met, she found a way to know just about everyone. I saw her writing people's names down after she met them (because, she said, "I don't have a great memory"). Not just the famous doctors, or the nurses in charge or the consultants, but the cleaning staff, the workers in the kitchen, the people who cleaned the toilets, everyone. Every shift, she would come in like a warm breeze on a cool day and say hello to everyone, by name, and in a short time, was able to tell you where they lived, who they were married to, what they thought of their job, and if they felt appreciated. Everyone loved this student because she made them feel seen.

She did the same with the patients and their families, but it didn't stop with names. She was the first person to help the nurses change a bed, flush a bedpan, get a warm blanket for an old lady, help open the doors, volunteer to transport a patient to a car, clean up a mess, get a sad and burnt-out doctor that extra cup of coffee to get through a night shift. This "average student" wanted to learn everything, and asked lots of questions from everyone, from the world-famous doctors, to the bedside nurse to the cleaner who had worked there forty years. She helped the other students, organized study groups, arranged thank-you notes at the end of their rotation for all the people in the department. None of this was done with fanfare or to make a scene, it was from a place of really wanting to be part of a team, and she genuinely saw everyone in the department as part of the team.

This extraordinary person was an average student by the typical definition, but she left us all feeling, *We must have her join us!* She inspired a sense of purpose and joy and, at the same time, was so teachable, so loved to learn, that by the end of her rotation her knowledge and understanding of the department was second to none. She went on to join our residency and in four years graduated at the top of her class. Now, over twenty years later, she leads her own department and every single person in it considers her one of the best and smartest doctors they have ever worked with. Not bad for an average student.

Far from being a one-off story of an exceptionally average student, this had been a recurrent theme through decades of working with students and residents. *Good average* is a key feature of the best students we look for in medicine and in life. That person who feels average, and because of it is much more open to being taught and being part of a team, always turns out to be, over time, the best physician, nurse, medical care provider. In other professions and trades, I hear the same thing over and again. Bring me your average and ready to learn over your exceptional know-it-all. Yes, there is that rarest of species, the exceptionally smart, exceptionally teachable, exceptional human. The team player who cares for the group more than their own accolades, who is also an outstanding student. That person can become quite exceptional, as long as they show some humility and understand there is always more to learn and always someone smarter, they will have a long and successful career.

If you are a leader, a teacher, a professor, a manager or employer, I implore you to consider the average candidate and look beyond their average resumé. If that average person understands the power of being good, kind, concerned, then they can become a superhero. Some people are modeled these traits by great parents and teachers so they come by it easily, while others with less supportive backgrounds have to work hard at it. For most of us, though, we might never be able to memorize PIE to the 48th digit, but we can hand a turkey sandwich to a tired, hungry, or scared fellow human and make their day. If you are average, you can become exceptional with a little kindness, openness, and enthusiasm.

The G Factor

THERE IS ANOTHER QUALITY I'VE learned to look for in otherwise average people, one taught to me by a colleague who ran their own company filled with some of the most exceptional people I have ever worked with. I call it the *G factor*.

Over a long period, we have worked with a technology company that has built out our education platforms to an industry leading standard and created a set of tools that make us not just an education company, but a leading technology think-tank company. This company is run by some of the best, kindest, most wonderfully average people I have ever met. The relationship has worked so well because they view the world in the same way we do, which is that the work, what it means in the world, is more important than the money. Money is important, people need to be paid, kids need to be sent to school, retirement accounts need to be funded and mortgages need to be addressed. After that, however, there is a very poor correlation between income and happiness. In fact, it tends to go down after a person has achieved that comfortable income.

With this concept in mind, I asked our colleagues in the tech company: Besides offering a competitive salary and good benefits and a really good job, what should we be doing? Our stated employee hiring philosophy, as I've mentioned, was to bring us your average, enthusiastic, teachable and we will do the rest. My colleague said they added one more thing to this list of requirements—what I call the G factor—that changed the long-term quality and happiness of the company and the people in it. That quality was a *global view* of the world. Stated another way, a desire to do good in the world. People who are average, hard-working, smart, humble, and who also care about others, the planet, and the plight of those less fortunate, are the best people to work with.

I find it disturbing that in some corners by certain people, having this global view of the world is considered weakness. These tend to be the same people who want to always be first, always get the credit, and don't have a sense that just being middle class in the West makes them extraordinarily privileged. Frankly, they are hard to work with. The G factor filters out people who are all about themselves, who always seem to turn a great team into a bad team. Those with the G factor have a more global perspective and thus appreciation. They look at the heroin addict, the homeless alcoholic veteran, and think, *A few less good choices and that could be me.*

Someone with the G factor understands that it is by sheer luck that they were born in a place that is stable, prosperous, and full of opportunity, and they are thankful for it in the deep-down places of their soul. They understand that most people in the world are born into exceptionally difficult circumstances, surrounded by war, famine, abuse, neglect, with no chance of schooling, no handed-down wealth, no security. And that it is chance, not drive, looks, or smarts, that caused them to be born on the "right side" of the tracks.

Once we incorporated an understanding of the G factor into our hiring, our already remarkable and dedicated team became even more exceptional (in part because we had already incorporated the G factor without explicitly knowing it most of the time). Now, with this extra layer of understanding, the addition of the "look for the G factor," we have a great algorithm for hiring. The traits we now look for include enthusiasm, desire to be part of a team, teachability, work ethic, shared vision, and the G factor. The beauty of these traits is that any average person can have, or develop them, they are independent of the school you went to or the scores you achieved or the family you come from.

The G factor is also a powerful way to find the people you want to spend time with. Two people in my life who have the G factor in hopeless abundance also happen to have G in their names: Father Greg Boyle and Geoffrey Kiplagat. One is a famous author, and beloved and world-renowned founder of the nonprofit, Homeboy Industries. The other is an average boy from Kenya, made an orphan at three, living in a mud hut, suffering from one of the most terrible conditions known to man, sickle cell disease. Yet this boy has a heart so big it becomes like a black hole, drawing people in and leaving them in awe of his goodness. Now nine as of this writing, G has a simple philosophy: "Be kind." There is no one kinder than G. You can read about him and the remarkable story of his family's life in the book I've mentioned earlier, *From Beyond the Skies.*

In medicine, it is easy to see a larger purpose, a grander goal, it is one of the gifts of the profession. In our education work, we get to teach people all across high income countries, and it is inspiring to see people learning from our excellent educators and platform. What inspires our people most of all, however, is our nonprofit arm. Many people, in many parts of the world, cannot afford to purchase our products. They need the information, desperately, in fact, so we created a nonprofit to deliver that information in a few simple ways: by giving away our product to students in low- and middle-income countries for free or at greatly reduced cost, and by asking our subscribers to help fund our work. The response has been amazing and the rewards outsized. Between donations made by our subscribers and those made by our company, we have been able to grant thousands of free subscriptions all over the world. Recently, we got a note from one of these students that, in part, reads as follows:

Here in Syria, we have very few resources, but your program has been such a blessing to us. To-

day we saved a child's life. He was unconscious and because of your program we knew what to do. There was a case just like this and a video of how to put in an IO line. We then pushed glucose and fluids and the child woke up. Without your help, without the free subscriptions you gave us, this beautiful child would have died.

Our internal bulletin board, after posting the above letter, was flooded with notes from our people saying how moving it was, how it made them cry, how it made them so proud and want to do even better so we could, as a company, give away even more. This same letter was sent with a video showing a team from this low-income country resuscitating the small child from the brink of death. Seeing it, our team lost it and the tears of joy and fulfillment were as great an expression of emotion about our work that I had ever seen.

The ripple effect of our commitment to the G factor does not end with free subscriptions. We have a group of high-income western doctors that travel the world and volunteer their time to teach other clinicians in low-income countries, though it no surprise that our doctors find they learn as much as they teach. We never have a problem getting teams filled with doctors and nurses to go to hard places, to give up thousands of dollars of income, and to simply serve, with the idea that everyone, all over the world, deserves excellent emergency care.

By incorporating the average good and G factor principles in our hiring, we have gathered a team that cares about people, about the world, and that draws gratification not so much from a salary and stock options as from the very work itself. I cannot tell how inspiring these wonderful people who work in our little company are to me and to each other. While we do not expect everyone to be a "bleeding heart do-gooder," we do avoid those people who show no interest in global compassion. I will say it again: there is extraordinary power in being average, and there is extraordinary power in compassion.

The Ripple Effect of Compassion

MANY YEARS AGO, I WORKED at a large hospital in Australia. It was early in my career and I was very impressionable. I was working in the Emergency Department and was struck by the fact that some patients would come in *every day*. One such patient was a gentleman called Rick. Every single day he would present with some complaint: chest pain, abdominal pain, headache. Coincidentally, every time he presented, he was drunk and wanted a free lunch and a bed to sleep in. This was seen by some of the staff as an abuse of the ER, and it drove many of the doctors and nurses crazy, especially in a city that had pretty good homeless services. Sometimes Rick would present very intoxicated, even semi-comatose, as he suffered from chronic and quite severe alcoholism. Often, upon sobering up, he would quite literally add insult to injury by insulting the staff. He was exceptionally difficult to work with and many staff tried to avoid him at all costs.

In that same ER was a charge nurse named Robin who oversaw the night shift. She was a rock in that department, had worked there for over thirty years, and was respected and feared by one and all. Not an inch over five feet tall, she towered over the place with her strength of will. One night, Rick showed up in bad shape. We had not seen him for a few days, which was very uncommon. He was covered in vomit, stool, and actual maggots. As you can imagine, the staff was repulsed; he smelled horrible and looked even worse. Robin, however, moved forward and took charge. Not by ordering the more junior nurses to clean him up, but by pushing Rick herself on the gurney to the shower area. There, for the next thirty minutes, she undressed him, removed the maggot-ridden clothes, showered him, shaved him, put him in clean hospital attire, and returned him to the ER to be seen by the doctors and staff.

When one of the other senior staff asked her why she did this, Robin replied, "As a leader you should be prepared to do the shittiest job in your department to show the staff no one is above the work." She went on. "And anyone can look after the clean patients, we're here to care for *all* the patients." To this day, thinking of her response keeps me humble. This leader earned the respect of everyone around her not by the way she used her power, but by the humility of her actions. It was her willingness to do the hard thing no one else wanted to do that made her a legend. Nothing superhuman, just *super average*.

I saw this same thing in different clothes many years later at another hospital in a county 8000 miles away and it was no less impressive. I was the senior resident in a large hospital in Los Angeles. It was a busy night with lots of patients and trauma victims but the team was humming along. I heard a commotion from one of the back rooms and went to investigate. There on the gurney lay an elderly white woman dressed in fine, expensive clothing with blood dripping from her hand after an unfortunate bagel cutting incident. Caring for her was a nurse and one of our remarkable medical techs, John, who, as it turned out, was the object of this patient's ire. Hearing her screaming that she did not want this "N-word doctor" touching her, I became enraged. John was a beloved figure in this ER, someone who had helped generations of young doctors and nurses survive in what can be an incredibly stressful environment. In the over forty years he had worked there, he had always been compassionate with the patients and nothing but exceptionally professional. To see him get called these names was too much for me.

John saw the look on my face as this woman continued with her tirade about the color of his skin and without a word, diffused the situation by silently stepping aside. I took a deep breath and turned to the woman, informing her that we didn't have white doctors or Black doctors at that hospital, we just had doctors, and if she wanted our help, she needed to stop with the bullshit. I actually cannot remember exactly what I said, but it worked as she calmed down and we got her stitched up and on her way. Later, I went to John and apologized for what he had been subjected to. Once again, the response has stayed with me for the rest of my career. He said, "It's okay, Mel, we have to look after all the people, even the ones full of hatefulness." It was not a platitude, not just a thing to say, this was how John chose to see his work, how he chose to live his life. In similar circumstances, I know I could never have been so unfazed by such hate and ignorance. Yet here was this proud, hard-working, exceptionally skilled man who saw his work more as more of a priesthood than a paycheck.

There was nothing exceptional about John, his past or his education. John was, by all accounts, an average guy. However, like Robin, it was his compassion, his understanding for other human beings, and his exceptional regard for his work that made him remarkable. They were just two average people doing anything but average work for people who didn't know or care they were in the presence of someone who transcended the reasonable, accepted title of "good" and moved on a whole other plane. The modeling of these two people showed generations of healthcare workers how to work and how to live. I would talk about these amazing people many years later in a variety of settings—with teams of doctors in hospitals, on conference stages, and in our educational videos—noting how their examples changed how I saw medicine and my role in it. Their actions made us all better doctors, because they showed us how it was possible to see the world and our patients through the lens of compassion, and you didn't need a shiny, hang-on-your-wall sign to be an exceptional leader.

I have also seen this remarkable compassion from my patients. One in particular who showed profound compassion at the end of his life was a man I treated in the 1990s, a time when every day you went to work in the ER you would diagnose multiple patients with HIV and AIDS, the final endpoint of that infection. It was a terrible time, young, otherwise healthy men and women being told they had an incurable disease and the road to their death would be lined with extreme suffering. It was the first, but not the last pandemic I would, we would all, live through.

Peter, a proudly gay, wonderful human was dying of a tumor in his chest brought on by HIV. The tumor was causing the lining around his lungs to fill with a blood-tinged protein fluid. As the fluid accumulated it would press on his lungs, taking up the space meant for those lungs, and he would get progressively more and more short of breath. He would then come to the Emergency Department where we would insert a needle between the ribs, through the muscle and chest wall, and put a plastic catheter in and drain out the fluid, often a liter or two. This would give him great relief but the procedure could be painful, very uncomfortable, and even dangerous if not done carefully. I performed this procedure on Peter myself a number of times and several times with the senior residents.

One night we had a medical student who was young and smart but had never done this procedure. I sheepishly asked Peter, this wonderful but very sick and dying man, if he would allow me to do this with the medical student.

Peter knew the dangers of the procedure and that having a medical student do it, even with a more expert person at their side, only increased that danger. I expected that he would kindly refuse as his days were numbered and this was not a risk he would reasonably want to take. To my surprise, delight, and forever wonderment he looked past me, stared right into this student's eyes, and said, "Of course, I wouldn't have it any other way. Let's get you trained in this procedure." Here he was, dying, in pain, so young and handsome, and in his last few days wanted only to show compassion for a student, to put himself at risk so that others might benefit.

The procedure went well and Peter was responsible for this student taking one giant step in becoming an expert in this life-saving work. Peter died a few weeks later from a pulmonary embolism, a clot that traveled to his lungs and allowed him to finally be at rest from that terrible disease. He was just a regular guy with a terrible disease, who in the last days of his life showed us what compassion looked like. He cared about this student, about me trying to train her, about the people she would go on and help if he did this thing. Peter, to this day I remain amazed at your strength, your compassion and your brave words and deeds. What you did that day, and indeed a few more times before you passed, really mattered. You, sir, really mattered and I am glad you are at peace but the world would have been much better if you had stayed longer.

These three people and their stories of exemplary compassion have stayed with me for decades. They have shaped me, my colleagues, and students because of the power their compassion showed. None of these people were anything but average, everyday folk, but the power of their compassion has been a bright shining light that lit up the lives of those around them and beyond. Compassion, even a little, can change lives and the best part is anyone can practice the skill. Any average person can become something more by simple kind acts and careful words. The Dalai Lama said, "Love and compassion are necessities, not luxuries. Without them, humanity cannot survive." I would add compassion is a superpower we all can wield; it makes us heroes, and it makes us human.

The Toxic Leader and the Death of all That is Good

IF BEING AVERAGE, KIND, CONCERNED, and a global thinker is important in an organization, it is no less important at the top. Put the wrong person in charge and they can, like a spreading cancer, undo the work of many exceptional people. Let me share with you perhaps the worst example of what we might call the "anti-G factor." We might call it many other things, but we have to call it f@#king awful and a dangerously important cautionary tale.

Some years ago, I found myself in a department of medicine with some of the most wonderful and talented educators I had ever known, before or since. It was an inner-city hospital in a low-income area and the patients were wonderful—working class, family oriented, and just happy to receive medical care. Mixed in with the working poor were many patients with substance abuse, interpersonal violence, mental health issues, and homelessness. But the average patients we saw were a hard-working, solid, just-looking-to-help-my-family-get-by sort. Simply a joy to work for.

In this department, the current and prior leadership had used the principles we have outlined and taken a series of average and above average students and turned them into incredible doctors, residents, then amazing faculty and leaders. These were also people with the G factor, a heart for the less privileged, an exceptional group and an exceptional place to work. There was a sense that we all were part of something extraordinary. Over time, the team here had developed an enormous amount of personal and corporate medical knowledge. The teaching rounds were open, accepting of questions, of junior learners and senior learners sharing their thoughts and experience. There was a real team approach to looking after these patients, who were also seen as part of the team. Truly a remarkable model.

In fact, this residency had become a focal point of education in medical education around the world. A world class department which students and faculty from across the county, and the world, were desperate to join. After graduation, the residents from this program could get jobs in any department, academic or private, in the country. Many of the best graduates gave up salaries that were two or three times what they could make working in this department to stay in this remarkable place. The mission and the people were so wonderful that the best and brightest were prepared to give up enormous personal benefits to be part of this team. The leaders of this department created this community by demonstrating it themselves. They were the best clinicians, the most compassionate, the best educators, the nicest people, the best researchers, and they had a most global mindset.

One of the most famous professors in medicine, known throughout the world, with multiple publications and textbook chapters and international speaking engagements, worked in this department, seeing lots of patients with students of all abilities. This professor, unlike any other person I have seen in this role, would turn to a student and ask, "Well, what do you think we should do next?" Not in an aggressive "let me show you how smart I am and how dumb you are" interaction. Just the opposite, a really heartfelt "you are part of the team." And it was a genuine question, believing they might have something to add that he had missed.

Then it all came to an end with such speed, such tragedy, that I still feel a combination of anger and extreme sadness. It all fell apart because of one person—well, actually two, but let's start with the first one. Toxic leadership took a blow torch to the place and burnt it down like some master villain from a Disney movie.

In this remarkable learning and service environment with thirty-plus faculty, one hundred-ish residents, and hundreds of nurses, there were, of course, some people with their own issues that could be difficult to work with and who did not entirely buy into the mission. One faculty member in particular had been there a long time, and desperately wanted to be in charge, to become the chair of this great department. To those of us who worked with him and watched him over the years, it was clear why he wanted to have this position. It was not to be in service to the patients, to the faculty, to the teaching mission. It was to be in charge. To be the boss. To have that power and to yield that power however he saw fit. I knew this person well and, while I am no psychologist, believed him to be a truly broken person. A person whose father was successful in medicine to the extreme and, I guessed, wanting to be the boss, be seen as the boss, was important in this man's life to "make daddy proud." This I can understand as I myself have suffered from this. What I cannot understand is why some people get their joy from putting other people down, by showing people that they are in charge and you are nothing.

This man delighted in tearing down students in front of patients, nurses, and other doctors. Not just simple "I am smarter than you" sort of moments, but really abusive behavior. It had been so bad that in the past, he had been expelled from his own department and ordered to get anger management classes (they didn't work). Frankly, in any other place he would have been fired. As so often is the case, he was kept around because of his connections. His father was a powerful man, with lots of research money and sway in the medical school. His career was saved on many occasions because of this simple fact.

This man would not only abuse the students, but the residents, the nurses, the faculty more junior than him and even the patients. He created an atmosphere of fear, dread, and the knowledge that no matter what you did, he would find a way to tell you, and anyone present, why it was wrong, to make you feel as low as possible. During this reign of terror, we lost some of the best students that rotated with us. So many times, we heard, "I would love to come to this place and train for the next four years, but I cannot be in a place with that guy in charge."

Eventually, he got the top job. The person in charge over this department and the dean of the medical school at the time was an even more toxic human than this man (an entire other story that has been documented in national newspapers). He granted our protagonist the position of department chair, despite all the faculty's concerns. Within eighteen months, the best faculty had left, students stopped matching us, the mood in the place had turned depressing and toxic, and the department was like a fire-devastated forest. Within two years, he was fired from the position. Not even the power of his father could save him this time. Too many lawsuits, too many residents complaining to the national accreditation body, too much money at stake for a hospital that was threatened with losing federal funding unless he was removed. This tremendous, almost mythical training ground had been destroyed by one very toxic and well-connected leader. It was one of the saddest, and most educational, experiences on the power of leadership I have ever seen.

Look out for these people; do your best to ensure they will not lead your group. Do not believe, as many in our department hoped, that once this kind of person gets the power they so desperately crave, they will become magically secure and a team player. This kind of egotism and flaw cannot be fixed with more power. There is no end to the black hole. No matter how much is given, more will be extracted. We've seen it play out on a grand scale in recent years in our politics and throughout history. To see it up close and personal on a much smaller scale was, however, a real revelation to me. Leadership matters. Sometimes we think leadership is so far removed from the day-to-day that it becomes almost irrelevant. It matters, it trickles down and sometimes it comes down like a deluge, a flood of biblical proportions.

When you look for leaders, look for the average, look for the G factor. The superstars from the big university with all the degrees and prior experience who plan to conquer the world are great. But I want that average person, the one who can relate, the one who shows humility, hard work, empathy, enthusiasm, kindness, and has a global heart. That's the person who will guide your group to be their best. Allow the group to be more than the sum of its parts. Inspire you all to punch above your weight class. They create a virtuous circle of wanting others to do well, of being part of the team. They measure their success not by personal accolades, not by power, but by the success of the group. They are average people who want everyone to be their best, and because of this, they are anything but average. They are extraordinary.

The Why and the Money

IN ANY BUSINESS, ANY VENTURE, any life goal, it is important to understand the *why*. The why is the key to any success. The why doesn't have to be all lofty and otherworldly, it can be simple, even simplistic. Without it, you will be like a ship without a rudder, any wave or wind will send you off course, or threaten to topple you. It is the power of the average person to achieve great things if the goal is clear and the method methodical. I have found it better to have an average goal, one you believe in, one you can stick to, one you can reasonably achieve, than to have a lofty goal you don't actually have the stomach for.

We decided early on that our why was pretty simple: to create an independent medical education without funding from third parties, like drug companies, and make it exceptional. It is a travesty in the world of medicine that the idea of being independent of third parties has been lost. Most institutions, companies, and individuals think they can take any manner of funding and gifts from the pharmaceutical industry then tell themselves, and the rest of us, it will never affect their practice or their recommendations. They are professionals, above such things, how dare you even suggest they might not be? Well, I know a few million (billion) reasons why they are *not* above it.

The pharmaceutical industry is not stupid. The reason they spend billions of dollars on prescribers is to help them "see the world" their way, and it works. Billions of dollars spent on clinicians, medical societies, and academies—the amount of funding for these great institutions of medicine from the pharmaceutical industry is truly mind-boggling. It occurs a little less now than it once did as the industry has determined an even better way of selling their wares, by going directly to the public, with direct-to-consumer advertising. Never fear, however, there is still a very good chance that that esteemed big university has, at some level, been bathed in the money of industry.

Don't get me wrong, we all need money, most of us want more of it, are happy to work hard for it, but it can also be a dangerous thing. To believe that someone, some group, can give you large sums of it and it not affect your work, voting, mindset, bias, is sheer ignorance. You can find many research papers just in the field of medicine that demonstrate that money works. It changes the way clinicians prescribe, the way they practice. Sometimes this can be good, often it is not. So, it is not because we feel superior to anyone else that we decided to not take any money from any out-side group, no advertising, no grants, no sponsorship, no nothing. It is precisely because we felt we were not above being manipulated that we rejected it.

The human is a curious creature; we need to believe we are good and upright. I know of no person, even the bad ones, who consider themselves "bad" and are okay with it. We all rationalize our bad behavior, in order to not feel so bad about ourselves. The logic goes something like this: I stole that lollipop not because I am bad, but because I really needed it. I have no money and the store-keeper is rich and will never miss it. I went to the fancy dinner and ate the pizza and donuts from the pharmaceu-tical representative with the great cheekbones, but I really do think their drug is the best. I have not been manipulat-ed. Actually, I manipulated them. I was going to prescribe that medication anyway, and those suckers gave me all this free stuff that didn't change a thing. *Right.*

We have, as a company, a great fear that medicine is easy to get wrong. It is complicated; humans and disease are complicated. You can be so sure you are right, and still be very wrong. So, the less bias you have the better. Let me give you a pretty famous example. Magnesium, that benign little element found in food and rocks and space and in you, was believed back in the 1990s to sig-nificantly reduce a person's risk of death if given to pa-tients having a heart attack.

Better still, magnesium, unlike so many drugs in medicine, was cheap, like dirt cheap. Imagine our excitement when we believed we had found a simple, cheap therapy that could save thousands, even millions of lives. We didn't just *think* it would work, we hoped and dreamed it would work.

The first studies, small, non-randomized, looked fantastic. The excitement grew. More studies came, randomized this time but small, suggesting up to a fifty percent reduction in mortality from heart attacks by the simple addition of this element to the IV going into the patient's arm. Some were skeptical, but most of us were on board and started using the treatment. Then came the first large study out of Europe and, guess what, it worked. Not as well as in those first studies, but a twenty-five percent reduction in mortality. This was good news, a much larger study and the magnesium was working, not as well as we thought, but working. I, we, all of us gave it to more people, convinced we were on the cutting edge, giving our patients the best care possible.

Then came a huge study, a well-designed, multi-country study involving tens of thousands of patients and . . . it didn't work. No effect of magnesium in the patients having a heart attack compared to the patients given a placebo. This was by far the biggest and best study to date. We could not believe it, so we didn't. Our reasoning was it *must* work; therefore, you must have done something wrong. You must have given it too late; if you had given it early, like in the first four hours, then you would have seen how great it is. So, the study was reanalyzed to see the effects in the first four hours and, again, it didn't work. Then more studies came and confirmed the results, leaving us with, how do I say it—magnesium all over our faces. We had been giving a treatment that didn't work. The only good part of this story is that the use of magnesium in heart attacks didn't seem to hurt anyone *and* its use stopped almost overnight.

This is unusual. Normally, if a new drug is found not to work, we—that is, industry or industry sponsored physicians—keep trying to *make* it work. With magnesium, the difference was that no one was making any real money on it, so it was no big deal to stop using it. In similar cases with expensive drugs for which, over time, the evidence becomes overwhelming that it had little or no effect, or an effect was outweighed by price and side effects, those drugs still get used. They get used because there is an enormous incentive to believe that they work. The data was "tortured" to try and find someone, anyone, in whom it might work and use that as an excuse to go on selling it. Money is dangerous in medicine. It provides an enormous incentive to believe what you really want to believe. Add to that clinicians wanting to help patients with a magic cure and you have a recipe for disaster.

In order to reduce our mistakes, we decided to not take outside money. If we got something wrong, it was not going to be because we had allowed money to cloud our thinking. There's enough difficulty getting it right in the field of medical education without that added filter. We decided to use a subscription model: the user pays a fee, they get content as free of bias as possible. No ads, no "grants," no research money, just the best review of the data as we can give. No doubt, we are not perfect, just a little less biased than some others. Money can corrupt in many other ways as well: it can make you forget who you are, why you do what you do. The love of money might not be the root of all evil, but it has to be up there.

For the average person to achieve great things, the goal must be clear and unclouded by bias, the work methodical, the patience great, and the team hand selected with like-minded souls. Do all this and it is hard *not* to achieve.

Death: The Greatest Average-Maker of All

DEATH, IN THE END, MAKES us all average. No matter how much money you make, no matter how great the achievements, death gets us all. It does not care how bright you are, how handsome, it doesn't even care how young you are. Once it decides to come, it comes. It is the great equalizer, the greatest "average maker" of them all. What we do with that knowledge can, again, make us more than average.

One evening, I was working in the Emergency Department and we got a call from a very distressed doctor from a small hospital nearby. I was the in-charge doctor at the large university hospital that night so the call came to me. I knew the doctor; he had trained in our department a few years before. He was all apology and energy and anxiety. "I'm sorry Mel, I'm sorry," he started, "I just sent you a dying baby. I did not go through the right channels, I just had to get him out of here to give him a chance." To transfer a patient from one hospital to another requires a series of phone calls, FAX's, and signatures, all appropriate to make the system work, but time-consuming and sometimes, rare times, that delay might be lethal. "I think he's bleeding to death. I put in some lines, gave blood and intubated him and sent him over right now via ambulance. I think he has an intraabdominal bleed, maybe from child abuse, I don't know, but they will be there soon. I am so sorry. I didn't know what else to do!"

As I was assuring him not to worry, that he did the right thing, the doors of the Emergency Department doors smashed open with two giant paramedics wheeling in a tiny child on a gurney. We transferred him to our hospital bed while the paramedics told much the same story as the doctor had a few minutes ago on the line. The mother then said she had been feeding the baby and heard a pop come from the child's belly and he went limp so she called 911. I had never heard anything like this. I dismissed it, and her. I was sure this was a case of child abuse, and assumed she was the abuser or covering for an abuser.

When we turned to the child, we indeed found a dying infant. Pale, fast heart rate, limp. The belly was tight, an ultrasound was done but not helpful. Blood was going into the child's leg bones via intraosseous lines that would then transport it back to the circulation and the heart. We decided to put a needle into the child's belly to see if it was, in fact, full of blood. The needle was placed and out poured bright-red, life sustaining blood. It was terrifying. The trauma surgeons had been called and were at bedside. Within minutes, they took the child to the operating room. The child would die a few hours later. This baby, this night, this terrible event, has stuck with me for decades now. Stayed with me, haunted me, for all that was done right, and for all I did wrong.

What was done right was the child was taken immediately to the closest hospital. What was done right was that the doctors there had trained in Emergency Medicine at one of the finest institutions in the world. What was done right was this amazing doctor and nursing team with limited resources made the correct diagnosis, put in lines, gave blood, put in a breathing tube and transferred the child to another, bigger hospital in about fifteen minutes. What they did is the stuff of legend. They gave this child every possible chance of survival. What was also done right was the university hospital team worked fast to confirm the diagnosis. A crack surgical team took the baby to the operating room within minutes of arriving in the Emergency Department.

Yet, despite their collective skill, death came. It turns out, this poor, sweet child had an abnormal artery in his abdomen. It was large and dilated and, on that night, in that mother's arms, it ruptured with an audible pop. It poured this innocent's blood into its belly at a rate faster than it could be replaced. In the world's medical literature, we could only find three other instances of this being recorded.

What went wrong was me. I broke the most basic rule of medicine: I presumed the worst, without fact, without humility. I assumed this poor mother had done something terrible. I had seen many horrible cases of child abuse in my career and, here again, I assumed, was another one. I did not yell at this distressed mother, I did not accuse her, I just ignored her. At the worst time in her life, moments she will never forget, no doubt moments that will torment her forever, I was not there to hold her hand, to give her comfort. I failed. When death came, I did not stop to soften the blow. I failed. For this mother, in those crucial moments, I was a far less-than-average doctor.

I learned a valuable lesson that night. I learned, yet again, to never assume, to always put the patient and family first, to never judge until all the facts are in, and even then, to have compassion. I have since told this story to many thousands of doctors and health care workers so they would not make the same mistake. It is little solace for my great failure.

Let me tell you another profoundly sad but important story involving death. Like most of them, this one happened at night. A thirty-two-year-old woman was brought to the Emergency Department with her husband, tiny daughter, and mother. This beautiful woman was near death, dying of breast cancer. The cancer had been treated and retreated; it had regressed and had returned. It was now in her bones, her brain, and in her blood. Her husband and mother had brought her to the Emergency Department because her breathing was irregular, and while they had hoped to care for her at home until she died, they had, in their words, "panicked" and come to us.

After our assessment, it was clear this was the end. Her records showed the cancer could not be stopped, it had spread and taken over her entire body. She was, indeed, breathing her last few breaths. Her husband's face streaming with tears told us of a wonderful wife and mother who had suffered so very much these last few years. He told us of all the people who dearly loved her. Tried to understand why God would take this extraordinary person from the world so young. She had made the life of everyone around her so much better. *Why her?* He was torched by the sadness of it. The hopeless pain of having to watch someone so good, so loved, die so young.

We told him there was nothing to be done, that we could make her comfortable with some more morphine but it would, in all likelihood, stop her breathing. Then, in a moment I will never forget, could never forget, he turned to his wife, kissed her beautiful bald head and said, "I love you so very much, but if it's too much and you have to go, it's okay, you can go now." A few hours later, she died with her family at her side and not a dry eye in all the department. Not one heart unbroken for all of them.

Death, in both of these cases, came too soon, too painfully. I fucking hate death when it does that. When it comes in one's ninety-eighth year, to a body that is worn out, a brain that no longer even knows its own name, when it comes at those times, it is a sad but compassionate messenger. When it comes too soon, it is cruel, reminding us again that, in the end, when it is time, no god or person can stand in the way. An old professor of mine used to say, "None of us is getting out of this alive." It is both a funny but deeply profound statement. If the average person understands that their life is temporal, passing, they have at their possession all the reason and energy they need to live an extraordinary life.

Those of us witnessing this young woman's death in the ER that night knew she was so very loved. Clearly, she had spread love and left love behind. It hurt so much because her life meant so much to the people she left behind. It does not take a philosopher to understand this. A life of love is a life worth living, no matter how long it lasts. If you live knowing that death can come at any time, your average life can be extraordinary. Anyone, *anyone*, can unlock that deep secret. Stop for just a moment, each day, and imagine if it was your last. What would you like to say to those you love? How would you like them to remember you? What would you worry about, and what would you cherish? Death comes when it comes. You decide what your life means to those around you until then.

Transitions

THIS YEAR I DECIDED TO stand down as CEO of our medical education company. It was my choice, after twenty-three years running my company on the day-to-day, I felt we needed new blood, new direction, new energy. I have loved being the CEO, the "boss," the chief vision-maker. It has defined my life for all of these years, given me great accolades and bolstered my frail ego. There comes a time, though, when you have to ask, *Why am I doing this, and should I stop?* The ideas I had are now dated, the energy I had, while still there, is not that of my twenty-something self. For our company to continue, to improve, I have to step aside and let younger visionaries take the stand, take the spotlight, take the wheel. This transition, like all big life changes, forces me to examine my averageness in a new light, which has been a painful reckoning but also a liberating new beginning.

This break from being the "guy" at EM:RAP had to happen at some point. I have always thought it better to do these transitions a little too early than a little too late. I left clinical medicine while I was still really good at it, but had lost the fire. Those attending physicians that stayed too long were an insult to me. I never wanted to be that person. I feel the same here. I want EM:RAP to be young and dynamic and I lost the obsessive fire, or at least, the need for the obsession, and indeed, it was necessary for my health. It had become too much, too obsessive, too big, too slow. I felt I needed to go back in time to a simpler place where I was in charge of myself and not the complexity of a fifty-person organization with thousands of contributors. Of course, wanting something simpler means you must give up the biggest role, and therefore the spotlight and the ego of that role. You cannot do both—step away from the responsibility while still trying to call the shots. If you try, you will, very quickly, screw it up. Organizations need clear leadership, goals, and lines of communication. There cannot be two masters.

Even when you try not to be a distraction, you run the risk of being one if you stay too involved. Here's just one example: On our SLACK channel (internal communication bulletin board) we review new procedure videos. This is important peer review, to make sure what we are showing is correct, both technically and from a production point of view. After I stepped down as CEO, I made the comment "great video" on a video that was posted, as a word of encouragement. Later, the new CEO wanted to make some improvements but the creator came back with, "Well Mel likes it, so I think it's fine as is." I never intended for my words to be used to short stop the peer-review process, but this is the problem of the long shadow and the "who's really in charge" question. Distance and role defining are important; beware the long shadow.

To those who have to do it next, or are already doing it, I say this: Do not expect it will be easy; if you do it at the right time, it must by definition, be extremely hard. The question of whether to go and do something completely new, leave the old completely behind, or return in a new, diminished role and help out the new crew without the shadow is a tough one to wrestle with. Either way, there needs to be a time away, a time to let the new tree grow its roots. The old saying is true, graveyards are full of "indispensable" people! Do not try to be indispensable, try to be a great leader, and transition off the power and be humble enough to let it happen. And if it comes with feelings of sadness, depression, loss, grief, regret, second-guessing, then it's probably the right time. A little too soon rather than a little too late.

The old saying, "If you love somebody, set them free" is true in business too. I love my company, the work and the people in it. Getting out of the way in order for it to continue to thrive, grow, and be a force for good, is the hardest thing I have done in my professional life, even more difficult than leaving my Emergency Medicine clinical practice. Where I stop and the company starts is completely unknown to me. I am my company and it is me. Knowing it's time to surgically remove myself from the day-to-day running of this great institution with all of its wonderfully average people feels hard. It feels like the beginning of being forgotten.

So, what does one do with these feelings? I can think of three things. I can reinsert myself and turn the spotlight back on to me. Or I can let it go, accept that this is what needs to happen, admit that there needs to be a clear and present change. The new guard must take the stand and establish their place as the new leader, and that can't happen if the old guard stands behind them, casting their shadow. It would be too easy to say, "We're still here, look at us!" The third option is to remain involved but not cast a shadow. This is, of course, the best and hardest of all the options. Finding that balance between wanting to help but not distract is something I now struggle with mightily. The whole process feels like a death, or the end of a wonderful marriage, like a sad divorce.

It should come as no surprise, then, that during the transition I became quite depressed. The *Who am I and have I screwed up my life?* thoughts tipped me into a very bad place. I wrote in an earlier chapter about my difficult childhood, and how I suffered from depression and even suicidal fantasies before, but this was worse. I saw my primary care doctor, a wonderful physician and woman I respect deeply, and we decided I should go on a medication for the short term. She specifically instructed me, "If you get suicidal thoughts, call me. Some patients starting these medications can develop suicidal ideation and it is very dangerous." So, I started the medications. Then it started.

Within a week I found myself having suicidal thoughts, fantasies. At first these were just fleeting moments, but over the next week, entire days became relent-less. I was convinced it would be best if I died because I was worthless to everyone and just a terrible burden. At one point I went for a walk and when I returned, my wife asked me what was wrong. I told her what I was feeling and broke into the most terrible sobbing, asking her to not hate me if I died by suicide. She was simultaneously deeply distressed, remarkably supportive, and clinically insightful. We called my primary care doctor who said to immediately stop those medications and come see her. I did, we changed the treatment, and the feelings went away within days.

I have cared for hundreds of patients with depression and suicidal thoughts. I have had friends, colleagues, and patients die by suicide. All those years, I could never quite understand how people could do that, how they could feel so bad as to not want to live. How they could be so selfish to their family. Now I know they were not being selfish. Now I understand that in these dark places, it is about wanting to lift the burden from those you love. You find yourself with such self-loathing you are absolutely convinced your family and the world would be better off without you. You feel that if this is what life is like, life it-self must stop, it is too much. I understand those feelings now in a deep and terrible way. I think of my friends Paul and James who died by suicide so young, so smart and caring, and only now all these years later do I understand. What a horrible disease, what a lying, horrible disease.

I do not like that I had this episode, it is difficult to share, but having gone through it I am more convinced than ever I'm just an average person experiencing what lots and lots of others have gone through. So, I write this as therapy and also as a kind of guide for anyone facing this. There is hope, there is treatment, you can live, you should live, you must live. Let those around you help you believe that. Here in the United State, the suicide prevention line is 988. If you are suffering with these same feelings I described, even as you're reading this, put the book down and pick up the phone, there are people ready to help. The feeling passes—your brain is lying to you—don't act, get help. We need you here with us. You're just average, just like the rest of us, and you are wonderful because of it.

Once you get through the darkest part of depression, you can see that it is what you do next that really matters—the reinvention of the self. If you're like me, you need to be busy, stay busy. Find a new hobby, a craft, a sport, or even a new business. If for you, retirement is sitting at the beach and reading all day, I applaud you! That is not me, nor is it most type-A individuals I know. Though it's hard for some people to understand, one of the things I get most joy from is reading scientific papers, summarizing them, writing summaries of them, and presenting them. My therapist had the insight that what I just described is, for most people, the *worst* part of their college experience. My friends and colleagues cannot imagine what my problem is, and wonder why I'm "still working." But it's not work to me, it's a hobby, it's meaning. This is retirement. It has been a great lesson, not imposing my values onto others as they have done to me.

A dear friend keeps asking, "Must you stay so busy? Why, even after all this time, do you feel compelled to start all these new projects?" My answer is inadequate but honest: I don't know, exactly, but to not do so feels wrong, uncomfortable. Not in the sense that I'm substituting one compulsion for another—it's not causing stress, anxiety, or disturbing those closest to me like an obsession. Rather, it's about being free to be who I really am. To explore all the things that interest me, and to rediscover my own "averageness" with a dose of humility and gratitude.

This is what I am learning, this is what I am allowing myself to be in this season of life. This is also the message we hear from the people and groups all around us: *I am harming no one, so please, let me be me so I may live this simple life my way, in my fashion.* And isn't this the great gift we can give one another? The freedom to be our uniquely average selves, pursuing what makes us happy and gives us purpose and meaning? Nothing profound here that has not been said a million times, by a million people, but it sure feels profound when you learn it for yourself.

What You Do Matters

EM:RAP Support inbox, Sept. 2023

Hi, I'm an ER doc at a critical access hospital in Vermont.

Long story short, I truly believe that EM:RAP has impacted my life in a huge way and I am emailing to communicate my deep gratitude for what you created. I have always approached the [medical profession with self-deprecation, empathy, and humility (and a touch of imposter syndrome) - lives are literally at stake, it's a chaotic environment, there is more to know than any one person can reasonably wrap their head around, and we are often swimming against the current in a less than optimal medical system.

I graduated residency in 2007 and for the first half of my career going to work was uniformly accompanied by a dose of dread and a pit in my *stomach. In short, being at work felt out of control. I considered leaving the profession on multiple occasions. I have been an EM:RAP subscriber for many years now and during that period I have listened to every single chapter of every main episode no less than twice. I have also consumed countless C3's and videos. Knowledge is power and the knowledge I have gained from EM:RAP has allowed me to overcome so many of my anxieties around work. EM:RAP has enabled me to finally believe that I am good at what I do. It has allowed me the feeling that I have a semblance of control while at work. It has allowed me to overcome situational insomnia the night before an early shift, to drive in to work without a sense of dread.*

Having access to the "EM:RAP universe" has literally changed my life - it has been transformative in that I have turned all that knowledge into the power to find some level of peace with my work. For that, I owe you (and everyone at EM:RAP) a deep debt of gratitude. Just wanted to say thank you :-)

Warmly,
Saul Nurok, M.D.

Several years ago, at the close of one of the monthly education shows for our series *EM:RAP,* I told the audience what they were learning was important because

"What you do matters." It's a pretty easy sell to a group of ER docs whose work literally reduces suffering and death on every shift. However, I believe this to be true no matter what your job: it matters, you need to understand that, accept that, and be as good at it as possible. Whether it's treating patients in the Emergency Department, cleaning plates, or flying airplanes for a living, it matters to us who do the work, and it matters to the people who experience our work. The average person needs to know that their work is worth doing. If they can find meaning in the work, they will do it far better than if they cannot. It's the same in all cultures, at all levels. If each of us does work that is meaningful to us, then that effort is meaningful, and our lives are meaningful.

If we, as average people, live out our day-to-day lives with this understanding, we are so much the better for it. We have a special empathy for people when we understand that we are all, by probabilities, average, trying to get by, with the gifts we have been given. Yes, you might be a world-famous neurosurgeon, but I can tell you there are hundreds or even thousands of neurosurgeons technically just as good as you. If you acknowledge that fact, there is a humility that should come with it. With that humility, I believe, comes compassion for those around you because you recognize you are not so different from them. That person who is drug addicted, homeless, and struggling is probably not so different from you. A few missteps, a different childhood, a slight mutation in a gene, and you could be right along with them. A little help and they can get back on track. The difference between the grandly successful and the gravely disabled is not so great as many believe.

I am both immensely proud and profoundly humbled by the fact that our medical education programs are used in over 160 countries across the world through our for-profit company and nonprofit program. They are used by clinicians and all manner of health care professionals to care for patients, to study for exams, to stay updated with new trends and practices and, I would even suggest, to be inspired. The key pillars of our success can be summarized in these simple principles:

1. Remember most people are average.
2. Repeat the key learning points over and again (see 1).
3. Make the material interesting and engaging as it helps with retention (see 1).
4. Remind people what they are learning is important and it matters.
5. Be humble, like, *genuinely* humble; you got here with help.
6. Remember what you do matters.
7. Understand being average is your superpower, most of us are average, and together we can be extraordinary.

Being average is not a bad thing, as long as you remember that you can move your average over time, be it in sports, business, life, anything. You can use the knowledge of being average to help yourself and help others to slowly but surely, move your game to a higher level.

This is, in fact, your power, even your superpower. Add to that superpower compassion, humility, and surrounding yourself with like-minded people who have the G factor, and great things are possible. I myself am gloriously average, our company full of marvelously average people. Yet, together, we have created a truly remarkable, meaningful, extraordinary business. We accomplished great things not in spite of our being average, but because of it. I hope you will, too, because anything is possible—even the most extraordinary things—when you embrace the wonderfully human fact that you are average.

About the Author

DR. MEL HERBERT IS AN emergency physician, entrepreneur, philanthropist, podcaster, and owner and former CEO of one of the most successful medical education companies in the world. He grew up in the Australian outback, went to medical school in Australia, and later emigrated to the United States. After completing his residency in Emergency Medicine at UCLA, he went on to become one of the most famous and awarded Emergency Medicine physicians and educators in the world. He has worked on the TV show *ER* and was featured in the documentary *24/7/265*. His educational programs have been downloaded millions of times in over 160 countries. The companies he started are valued in the tens of millions of dollars, and the team he helped gather has redefined medical education over the last twenty-five years. Most importantly, Mel Herbert is a father, a husband, and a very, *very* average guy.